THE BRITISH BUS STORY

Early 'Eighties

The Die is Cast

ALAN TOWNSIN

© The Transport Publishing Company Ltd April 1992

ISBN 0 86317 170 2

Photocredits

G. H. F. Atkins	6, 42(bottom), 49(top), 54(bottom), 61(upper), 73(top), 80(bottom), 81(top)	R. Marshall	3, 12(top), 24(both), 25(top), 29(top), 32, 33(bottom), 34, 35, 37, 41(bottom), 42(top), 44(top), 52(top), 55(top), 59(bottom), 60(both), 69(lower), 70(top), 75, 80(both top), 82(bottom), 88(all)
Bedford Vehicles	70(bottom)		
Bristol Coachways	23		
S. J. Brown	15, 54(top)	NBC/TOOC	19(bottom), 21, 26, 27, 29(bottom), 30(top), 33(top), 38, 39(bottom), 73(bottom), 76(all), 77, 78, 85, 86, 87(top), 91(top)
Cotter Tours Ltd	28		
DAF Bus	64	A. A. Thomas	6, 45, 48, 58, 68(bottom), 89
Excelsior Travel	71(top)	D. Wayman	7(both), 8, 9(both), 10(both), 11(top), 12(lower), 14, 16(all), 17, 18, 19(top), 20(both), 22, 25(bottom), 31(top), 36, 39(top), 40(both), 41(top), 43, 44(bottom), 46(both), 47, 49(bottom), 50(both), 51(bottom), 52(bottom), 55(bottom), 56(top), 61(bottom), 62, 63(both), 65(both), 66(both), 67(both), 68(top), 71(bottom), 81(bottom), 87(bottom), 90, 91(bottom), 92
Ford Motor Co	56(bottom)		
Max Fowler	30(bottom), 31(bottom), 53, 57, 69(top), 72(both)		
Michael Fowler	82(upper), 83		
Hestair Duple	74		
M. R. Keeley	84		
K. Lane	13		
Leyland Bus (courtesy BCVM)	11, 51(top), 59(top)		

Opposite. At the end of the 'seventies, new bus deliveries were being made on a large scale to most fleets. City of Cardiff Transport placed 97 Bristol VRT models in service beginning in December 1977, when the first of a batch of 26 with Willowbrook bodywork were added to the fleet, including No. 306, seen here against the impressive background of Cardiff Castle in August 1986. It is followed by No. 335, delivered in 1978 and representative of the balance, which had Alexander bodywork, and of which delivery was completed in February 1980. A further 64 new double-deckers were added to the fleet in the early 'eighties, typical of the level of fleet renewal then normal but rarely found since.

Designed, typeset and produced for the publishers by Mopok Graphics, 128 Pikes Lane, Glossop, Derbyshire Printed and bound in Great Britain

Contents

Introduction

A time for plain speaking

Looking back from the radically altered atmosphere of the bus industry of today, the early 'eighties are apt to seem no more than a prelude for what was to follow. That would be to under-value a great deal of effort put in to attempts to improve services and vehicles that were only marginally related to political events, as much of this volume endeavours to show.

Yet the fact remains that a small group of politicians, almost certainly a minority in the Conservative party as it stood at the time of its victory at the 1979 General Election, was determined to proclaim the twin themes of privatisation – about as ugly a word as its opposite twin, nationalisation – and deregulation, to a degree very few people other than the circle of close associates of the then new Prime Minister, Mrs Margaret Thatcher, realised.

There had been small but clear signs of what was in mind even before then when Norman Fowler, a loyal ally of Mrs Thatcher and 'shadow' spokesman on transport in 1978-79, outlined ideas about dismantling the road service licensing system which had been the foundation of the industry's structure since it was set up by the Road Traffic Act 1930. His appointment as Secretary of State for Transport led inevitably to the adoption of some of those ideas in the Transport Act 1980. However, the deregulation of express coach services, though controversial in theory, was for the most part widely welcomed in practice, largely because it lifted very severe restrictions that had resulted from the powers of objection, almost amounting to a veto, that had previously been given to the railways.

For a little while, it seemed as if further change might be handled in a more temperate way, underlined, so it seemed, by two successive appointments of men of more moderate views, David Howell and Tom King, to the post of Transport Secretary. Then in 1983, one of those ironic quirks of fate that can influence national as well as personal events completely altered the picture. The enforced resignation, because of a personal problem, of Cecil Parkinson from Mrs Thatcher's second Government led to a cabinet reshuffle and the appointment of possibly the most extreme Thatcherite disciple, Nicholas Ridley, as Secretary of State for Transport.

He lost no time in sweeping away previous confidential understandings that the National Bus Company would be privatised as a going concern and insisted that virtually unregulated competition was to be the watchword for the industry's future. The Transport Act 1985 was based on these principles and, almost as an aside, included provisions which discouraged such activities as joint operation, so often the logical way of running routes linking a locality served by one operator to that near another's base. Indeed operators were encouraged to take up aggressive attitudes to their neighbours and co-ordination became a dirty word. We were into an era of 'bus wars'. All this was supposed to give better service to the public.

In fact, the public has voted with its feet to the contrary, very often putting them to the accelerator pedal of its cars or reverting to trains after becoming fed up with repeated revisions of services when one or other bus operator has had to give up after a competitive battle. A recent survey of services in areas formerly served by Passenger Transport Executive buses shows that fares are up, drivers' wages down (both corrected for inflation) and the 4.5% rise in passenger journeys that had been achieved, partly by subsidised fares, in 1982-86, has given way to a fall of 20.6% in the period to 1990, despite an increase in bus mileage.

Had he troubled to find out, Mr Ridley could have been warned on the basis of history that this would happen, for direct competition of two bus services along the same route implies very expensive over-provision of service to attempt to attract the major share of custom and leaves both participants impoverished, one often fatally. Even the winner can suffer greatly. One former NBC subsidiary, Wilts & Dorset, admitted recently that bus wars from 'invasions' by previously friendly neighbours (also formerly part of NBC) had so damaged the company financially that it took

One of the most remarkable phenomena of the early 'eighties was the collapse of demand for the Leyland National, from a home-market peak of nearly 900 vehicles per year in 1978 to virtual extinction six years later. Among the last to be built for an NBC fleet were a batch of six with coach seating for Midland Red West dating from the spring of 1984, of which No. 1202 is seen in Birmingham. They were of the rare type built with Gardner 6HLXCT engines, an option introduced almost at the end of production but too late to stimulate demand. Even so, it seems incredibly wasteful that the Workington factory, one of the world's most impressive bus-building plants, should be so starved of orders for later Leyland models as to be on the point of closure as we go to press.

three years to recover, during which no new buses could be afforded. Much the same applies elsewhere and it is significant that the rare healthy new bus orders seen nowadays have mostly come from concerns strong enough not to suffer much competition. In the past, take-over or agreements have resolved matters, but under the new regime, operators seem to be condemned to a limbo of ever-present threat of near-destruction.

The catastrophic damage to British bus and coach makers is perhaps the most telling indication of the devastation that has been wrought. At the end of the 'seventies, over 5,000 new buses and coaches were regularly entering service annually in Britain, 95 per cent British-made. The Leyland group alone made 3,400 of these in 1979, in addition to as many exports. Last year, 1991, the total of full-sized buses and coaches registered in Britain was 1,871. That figure includes purpose-built midibuses but not van-derived minibuses, for which accurate figures are not yet available, though known to be much reduced from the temporary peak in the 1986-88 period.

The last Leyland factory – the Workington plant, specially built in 1972 – is about to close, the only 'ghost' of the Leyland name being the manufacture of the Olympian double-deck chassis now moving to Volvo's Scottish truck factory in Irvine – Volvo took over Leyland Bus in 1988. MCW, Leyland's strongest challenger in the early 'eighties, closed in 1988, a 'ghost' of its business similarly going to Optare, nowadays part of a group with DAF at its centre. Volvo, DAF and Mercedes-Benz (the most popular minibus make) are all well-run and responsible European concerns, but that does not lessen the tragedy for Britain. Fortunately, we do still have some British makers left – Dennis now has the only bus chassis works of any size (hardly huge, with 383 registrations in Britain last year) in England, and the only one British-owned. There are still a few good British bodybuilding firms – but how much of this shrunken industry will survive long enough to be still there when the penny finally drops that many thousands of new buses are urgently needed to revitalise the nation's fleet? All too often, passengers have to put up with tired vehicles that have been sold and resold several times and lack the comprehensive overhauls once standard practice in well-run fleets.

The new Government, of whatever complexion, must face up to the fact that deregulation has simply put Britain's once-proud bus industry into no better than a third-world league. Operators must be allowed better stability as a basis for investment – there might just be a time for British manufacturers to be able to begin bringing the fleets up to date if there is a change of direction now.

Steventon, 1992   Alan Townsin

This scene in Friary Street bus station, Guildford, in April 1985 was at that date superficially much the same as was to be found in the area of almost any National Bus Company subsidiary since the mid-'seventies. The Alder Valley Bristol VRT with ECW body departs on a local service under the watchful eye of an inspector standing alongside a Leyland National – both standard group vehicle types in the similarly standardised corporate livery, even if the advertising industry invention of the T-shaped format for the side advertisement on the VRT was a recent development which did nothing for vehicle appearance – in fact advertisements dwarfed the decidedly mean destination lettering. However, much more fundamental changes were firmly in the pipeline, for the Transport Bill which had been laid before Parliament in January of that year provided for the dismantling and sale of the State-owned NBC empire. By the end of 1987 Alder Valley, split into parts similar to the old Aldershot & District and Thames Valley companies from which it had been formed by merger in 1972, had been sold off, though the Aldershot area's vehicles retained the contrived Alder Valley fleetname. The VRT, No. 943, was one of 91 in the fleet with Gardner 6LXB engines dating from the late 'seventies and early 'eighties.

Chapter one:
The end of an era

Back in May 1967, Mr Moris Little, Chairman of the Scottish Bus Group but speaking in his capacity as Chairman of Council of the Public Transport Association and referring to the reorganisation of the bus industry then being planned by the Labour Government of the time, spoke of "sticks of dynamite which are to blow up the foundations of the industry". In the event, the resulting Transport Act 1968, though creating the National Bus Company and providing the basis for the Passenger Transport Executives, left most of the more visible parts of the industry undisturbed in terms of operating concerns. The names on the sides of the buses were largely unchanged, except in and around a few cities, even if the structure of the industry had altered significantly.

By comparison, the 'eighties really did bring revolution on a huge scale – this time the dynamite went off with a massive explosion. The Transport Act 1980 gave some indication of what was to come, even if the deregulation of coach services did not produce the victory for private enterprise expected. Yet even then, the magnitude of what

The coach side of the industry was the first to experience the change in political and economic climate, with Government encouragement of competition, even though the Transport Act 1980 impinged more directly on express services rather than tour operation. Glenton Tours had specialised in high-grade extended tours for many years, using vehicles painted in a very restrained beige livery. Dennis chassis had been favoured until the 'fifties, followed by a period of allegiance to the AEC Reliance, but in April 1974, a pair of Volvo B58 models, then quite rare in Britain, entered service; TME 129M seen here, still looking immaculate, in Bowness in June 1980, was one of them. Further Volvo coaches followed in subsequent years, and the switch from AEC to Volvo was not uncommon among independent operators, either voluntarily, or as a result of manufacture of AEC chassis ceasing in 1979. Plaxton 39-seat bodywork was fitted, the centre entrance, rare by that date, being a Glenton characteristic feature.

was coming was far from clear to people in senior positions within the industry– in fact one cannot help wondering if even the politicians about to play a crucial role understood the full consequences of putting their philosophy into effect in the way that was to unfold in the Transport Act 1985 and the sequence of events that followed.

In a parallel way, the bus and coach manufacturing industry was also to change almost beyond recognition. There had been quite a few closures of once-important factories before 1980, but the major British-owned concerns were virtually unchallenged as suppliers of vehicles used by British bus operators. Imported chassis and, to a smaller degree, bodywork, were beginning to take a sizeable share of independent coach operators' orders for new vehicles, but this had yet to spread, except on a very small scale, to

The most obvious legacy of the Transport Act 1968 had been the formation of the Passenger Transport Executives, that covering Manchester and its surrounding area being the largest. By the beginning of the 'eighties it was known as Greater Manchester Transport, building up a large fleet of buses to a uniform specification laid down by 1972 and having fleet numbers beginning at 7001. Seen here in Prestwich on a rainy day in March 1983 is No. 7150, the final vehicle of the initial batch of 150 Leyland Atlantean AN68 models, most of which had bodywork built by Park Royal though this was one of the final five of this batch bodied by Northern Counties. This latter concern was GMT's main bodybuilder and had become a subsidiary of that organisation.

other types of fleet.

The single event which set the scene for fundamental changes was the election of the Conservative Government under the leadership of Mrs Margaret Thatcher in May 1979. Yet even in 1980, the bus and coach industry was still remarkably similar in the face it presented to the public to that which had existed half a century earlier, despite a succession of Governments of varying political complexion and several important pieces of legislation. Quite often the same operator's buses, often of the same make, could still be observed on much the same routes and the boundaries of operating areas, usually the subject of formal agreements, were quite often unchanged.

The Road Traffic Act 1930 could almost be said to have frozen the *status quo* in existence at that time. That is an exaggeration, of course, but the road service licensing system the Act set up was, to some degree, based on 'grandfather's rights' – in other words the established operator on a specific route usually received the road service licence for that route and, in general, no newcomer would be allowed a similar licence. The converse of this was that the operator had to justify to the Traffic Commissioners set up under the Act any alteration in the service – most obviously, any increase in fares – they might wish to make. In the traffic courts set up to decide such matters, objections to the operator's proposals could be

heard, and among those who could lodge objections were the railways, which tended to take a very restrictive view of long-distance coach services in particular.

Hearings in the traffic courts were often quite fiercely fought – in the early days, quite eminent counsel were engaged to fight cases – and right up to 1980, an application for a fares increase had to be supported by detailed evidence of the increased costs on which the claim was based. Yet the general public for the most part knew little of such things, still less took up the rights they had to participate in the process. Local councils frequently did so, however, and operators used to complain with some justification of the time taken to overcome what they felt were unreasonable objections.

On the other hand, it was almost inevitable that the management of major operators and the chairmen of the Traffic Commissioners in the various official Traffic Areas became well-known to each other. The latter, often retired army officers, or people with a background in law, had a difficult job and set high standards of integrity. Yet it was understandable that independent operators sometimes felt that it was unreasonably difficult to obtain a licence, even for a new service which they might have identified as one fulfilling a need which existing routes did not meet. And the lack of direct public comment meant that such trends as the widening of headways as larger

types of bus were introduced were not challenged by people who probably rarely used the services themselves.

The whole set-up had been introduced on the premise, very much out of fashion nowadays, but widely accepted in 1930 and for many years subsequently, that competition is inherently wasteful when applied to public transport. No responsible operator intentionally puts on a service unable to cope with the numbers of passengers to be carried and on this basis a second, competing, operator implies over-provision. The writer used to somewhat mistrust the argument, especially when an independent operator wished to run a high-quality service or perhaps one at a lower fare than the local major operator. Yet recent experience of numbers of passenger-miles continuing to fall even though bus-miles have gone up under deregulation seems to support the basic viability of the point. Ironically, in these days of greater consciousness of global warming, pollution, etc, it seems to be largely ignored.

In effect, even though the Road Traffic Act 1930 had been succeeded by later Acts in many details, its essential provisions were still in force in 1980. There had been a great deal of unregulated competition in areas outside major towns prior to 1930, and the rapid growth of motor bus services, with numerous small firms running relatively nimble small-capacity buses, had produced a situation which was

Independent operators, particularly those running bus services, sometimes felt that the route licensing system was biased against them. The attitudes of neighbouring independent and publicly-owned operators to each other varied widely. In Staffordshire, there had been many disagreements and disputed applications involving Berresfords Motors Ltd of Cheddleton, near Leek, and its smaller associate W. Stonier & Sons Ltd of Tunstall in relation to the local NBC subsidiary, Potteries Motor Traction Co Ltd. Here EKR 154L, a Stonier Leyland Atlantean with Northern Counties body, is seen on a local service in July 1981. The vehicles had been new to Maidstone Corporation in 1974, but following the appointment of Alan Price to the general managership of that undertaking, also in 1974, a policy of using light Bedford and Ford single-deckers had led to the sale of double-deckers after only a few years' service.

generally agreed across widely-differing political viewpoints as being unacceptable. In towns and cities, forms of regulation were already old-established, often going back to Victorian times, when horse-bus competition had very soon given way to forms of licensing and control, generally under police control. When municipal tramways and, later, buses were operated the borough and city councils tended to protect them from competition, and this situation was continued after 1930.

Yet by 1980 circumstances had greatly changed. The huge growth in the use of the private car had led to reductions in frequency or complete withdrawal of some services. Reduced patronage meant fewer people to provide the revenue if services were to be run on a basis of them being expected to pay their way, and so fares tended to

rise faster than other items.

To a newly-elected Government of which the Prime Minister in particular considered that free competition was the answer to a wide range of problems, the stage was set for fundamental change. Even so, it was not until six more years had passed that a much larger charge of dynamite than that of 1968 was placed under the *status quo*.

In 1980, and indeed until 1986, there were four basic types of operator. What could still be called the area-agreement companies (for the agreements governing the boundaries of their operations generally continued to be observed) mostly still existed, very often retaining names that went back well before 1930. However, almost all had become part of the two major nationalised groups. The National Bus Company, controlling operating companies based in England and Wales

and operating 15,586 vehicles between them in 1980, had been formed as a direct consequence of the Transport Act 1968, but in effect it was a merger between the Tilling group of bus companies, which had been in State ownership since 1948, and the British Electric Traction group's bus interests in Britain, of roughly similar size, which agreed to sell out in 1967. In Scotland, the Scottish Bus Group's subsidiaries, with 3,718 vehicles altogether in November 1980, had been nationalised since 1949. (The full story of earlier stages in the respective stories of these groups and other types of operator since 1945 is to be found in other volumes of this series).

The Passenger Transport Executives (PTEs) were another creation of the 1968 Act. The original scheme was for bodies to be set up for designated areas surrounding certain major cities to be

Agreements defining the operating areas of adjoining major operators were almost always old-established. There was a certain irony in the painting of this Leyland National of Crosville Motor Services Ltd in the livery of Mid-Cheshire Motor Bus Co as a commemorative exercise in 1980, for it had been the purchase of Mid-Cheshire by the North Western Road Car Co Ltd in 1924 that had led the latter into conflict with Crosville. However, this was resolved by an agreement made between North Western and Crosville defining a boundary between each other's operating areas, signed in April 1925. In 1972 North Western's services in the area had been transferred to Crosville as a consequence of the take-over of most of North Western's services by the SELNEC Passenger Transport Executive.

The Scottish Bus Group, State-owned since 1949, had its origins in the group of operating companies built up by the Scottish Motor Traction Co Ltd in the 'twenties and early 'thirties. It had its own ideas on bus design, generally quite different from NBC, and continued to favour the mid-engined Leyland Leopard as a basis for many of its single-deck requirements right up to the early 'eighties, very often, as here, with Alexander bodywork. This example with Y-type 53-seat bus body was one of a batch for W. Alexander and Sons (Fife) Ltd and is seen in Edinburgh in September 1981, soon after entering service. The Fife company had been formed in 1961 when the operating area of the original Alexander company had been split – the latter had also once owned the bodybuilding business, but that became separate when not included in the sale to the British Transport Commission in 1949.

responsible for public passenger transport, on a two-tier basis. The Passenger Transport Authorities (PTAs), at first composed of representatives of the city and borough councils, were to be responsible for policy while the PTEs were responsible for operating services, initially with bus fleets taken over from those cities and boroughs in the area which had run their own municipal services.

At first there had been four PTE fleets, but two more had been created as a consequence of the reorganisation of local government in 1974 (which had also created the Metropolitan County Councils which took over the functions of the PTAs) and a seventh, covering the Glasgow area, was

added in 1975. In descending order of size they were Greater Manchester, West Midlands (centred on Birmingham), West Yorkshire (with Leeds as the largest city), South Yorkshire (Sheffield area), Merseyside (Liverpool etc), Strathclyde (Glasgow) and Tyne & Wear (based on Newcastle-upon-Tyne). Between them they were operating 10,479 buses in November 1980.

Very similar in status was London Transport, originally founded in 1933 as a self-supporting public body but which had been put under the control of the Greater

London Council in 1970. The London Transport Executive fleet was easily the largest owned by a single undertaking with 6,475 buses.

In 1980, there were still 49 bus fleets owned directly by local authorities. In England and Wales these were city or borough councils but in the three Scottish instances, the ownership had passed to regional councils covering much larger areas even though operation was almost entirely within a much more compact city area in each case. The combined fleet was 5,539 vehicles in November 1980, giving an average fleet size of 113 vehicles, though in practice this varied quite

The Passenger Transport Executives had begun by 'inheriting' the fleets of the municipal fleets in their areas. In the case of West Midlands, Birmingham City Transport had greatly outnumbered the others and its practices were often still very evident in terms of vehicle design, livery (apart from the use of a slightly lighter shade of blue than the very dark colour favoured by BCT) and such details as fleet numbering methods. Number 6474 was one of a series of 270 Daimler Fleetline buses with MCW bodywork built to the usual intermediate 14ft. 2in. height – again a BCT characteristic – favoured by WMPTE in the mid-'seventies. It is seen in West Bromwich in May 1980.

London Transport's bus fleet was undergoing a period of rapid change at the beginning of the 'eighties, when large fleets of models which had seemed desirable to the management when new were being discarded after short lives. The AEC Swift single-decker shown, SMS775, which had entered service in December 1971 as one of the final 100 of the 838 buses in the SM and SMS class, was one of the longer-lived of its type, having a few months short of ten years' service when withdrawn in 1981. The Leyland-built Fleetline, DMS2043, a Gardner-engined bus dating from January 1977, was to achieve only five and a half years of service in London when withdrawn in 1982, though many similar vehicles were to run far longer with their subsequent owners. Both had MCW-built bodywork and were photographed at Victoria in March 1980.

widely from the 601 vehicles of Lothian Regional Transport operating in Edinburgh, right down to the three small vehicles of Colwyn Borough Council. The formation of the PTEs had reduced the numbers of such fleets as well as causing the largest, such as the former municipal fleets of Birmingham, Manchester and Liverpool, to disappear – the largest English municipal fleet was that of 381 vehicles operated by Nottingham.

The fourth category of operator was the independent concern, and in 1980 this was still most typically a relatively small business, probably running coaches largely on private hire or holiday-related activities. Independent operators of bus services were to be found, sometimes in quite large numbers, in more rural areas and also in pockets often related to parts of the country where coal mining was still a major industry. But in many parts of the country, and especially within cities or the areas around them, independent

The direct local authority ownership of bus fleets was still a significant part of the public transport scene in many parts of the country, even though the numbers of such undertakings had diminished over the years. Still apt to be described in everyday conversation as 'Corporation buses', such fleets had often acquired different forms of official title. In Scotland, the three remaining municipal fleets were transferred to newly-formed regional councils in 1975 and so Aberdeen's buses, though still virtually confined to 'the granite city', were officially the property of Grampian Regional Council. This scene in late 1981 conveys the standardised nature of the fleet – batches of Leyland Atlantean AN68 buses with Alexander bodywork had been added regularly since the mid-'seventies, usually 20 per year and, by November 1982, Atlanteans accounted for 180 of the total fleet of 226 vehicles.

The typical independent operator was likely to be engaged in running coaches, rather than buses, in the early 'eighties, as had been the case for many years. Among the larger concerns was Grey-Green Coaches Ltd, based at Stamford Hill in the northern suburbs of London. Together with its smaller associate concerns Orange Luxury Coaches Ltd and World Wide Coaches, it was running 103 coaches and one double-deck bus in 1981, the latter an open-topper used for private hire. Its main traditional business had been in regular express services from London to East Anglia and seasonal routes to other seaside resorts, and though activities were changing, the switch to bus operation did not begin until 1986. Earlier in the 'eighties the fleet was largely composed of Leyland Leopard coaches, of which VLB 662M with Plaxton bodywork is seen in this June 1982 scene – EYH 811V with Duple body in World Wide livery is seen alongside.

Independent bus operators were rarely to be found in or near major cities in 1980, and indeed the trend towards their disappearance there had been in force for nearly 50 years. In some other parts of the country, matters were different, County Durham still being an area where relatively small bus-service operating concerns were numerous and often old-established. This collection of Leyland Titan double-deckers was seen in August 1980 at the premises of Weardale Motor Services Ltd in the village of Frosterley. All but one of those visible had been acquired second-hand, belonging to a batch of PD3/4 models with full-fronted Northern Counties bodywork originally placed in service by Southdown Motor Services Ltd in 1965, including BUF 276C, nearest the camera. Weardale had also bought new examples from time to time, these including 6 BUP, with Alexander bodywork, parked alongside.

bus services were very rare. The area agreement companies had generally followed a policy of buying out competitors when opportunity arose which went back to the days of the 'twenties. The Road Traffic Act 1930 had given more security to those concerns in business at that time but over the years many of them had sold out and even some of the older-established and more tenacious family concerns had given up, either when younger members of the family wanted to pursue other interests or when faced with what had seemed an irreversible trend towards public ownership of all forms of public transport.

There were quite a few exceptions to this general rule and, in addition, some private operators whose activities were purely on the coach side saw the possibility of getting a foothold in the

bus business as a result of the election of a Government more sympathetic to their type of business. However, the Transport Act 1980 gave the first opportunities for increased competition to those who wanted to operate their coaches on the longer-distance scheduled services, so there was still, at that stage, a continuation of the idea that an independent operator was more likely to be primarily involved with coaches.

The United Kingdom total of buses and coaches owned by all types of operator in 1980 was 71,256, of which about 42,000 were operated by one or other of the publicly-owned types of organisation described above. There were also Ulsterbus Ltd and Citybus Ltd, both State-owned organisations running buses in Northern Ireland, Citybus having taken over the former

Belfast municipal fleet, with 972 and 334 vehicles respectively. Isle of Man National Transport rather similarly ran services in that island with 82 buses. There were thus roughly 28,000 vehicles owned by independent operators in the United Kingdom, the great majority of which were coaches.

Most of the publicly-owned categories of operator also owned some coaches, particularly the nationalised company groups which had sought to expand their coach operations in an effort to counterbalance the falling traffic on bus services being felt by all categories of operator. There had been renewed emphasis on commercial operation even under the Labour Government led by James Callaghan in 1976-79, and this was intensified by the new-style Conservatives under Mrs Thatcher. The extent to which major

By 1980, one of the functions of the new bus grant scheme as originally set out in 1968 had been completed in many fleets – that of allowing the replacement of buses that were incapable of economic conversion to permit operation without a conductor. The Tilling group had continued to favour the front-engined Bristol Lodekka for its double-decker duties through most of the 'sixties, in some cases retaining the rear-entrance layout. The United Counties Omnibus Co Ltd was a case in point, and its last regular all-day Lodekka working was on a pair of local services in Luton. Number 713, an FS6G-type, waits at the terminus of service 21 in Sundon Park in October 1980. The high standards of maintenance of this ex-Tilling NBC company are conveyed by the turn-out of this fourteen-year-old vehicle – the Lodekka's rugged design and the exceptional fuel economy of the Gardner engine might have justified a considerably longer life, but the economics of a crew of two on a 60-seat capacity told against them.

change in structure was in mind had yet to become clear, but the intensified pressure to minimise subsidy and for services to pay their way was obvious almost immediately.

There was a steadily growing atmosphere of 'business' as opposed to the concept of public service as the primary aim which had been very strong in the public sector, especially the municipalities and their successors. Yet in many ways, older-established attitudes continued to prevail. There was still a sense of continuity and few people at any level in the industry yet had any doubt that its basic structure was set to continue unaltered in essentials under the new regime.

In particular, the ordering of new vehicles largely continued in the manner that had been usual in the 'seventies. This subject, like others touched upon in this chapter, will be examined in greater detail later in the volume. However, one aspect of Government policy was having a quite opposite effect to its long term consequence. This was the phasing out of the new bus grant which had been one of the new measures introduced as part of the Transport Act 1968. The aim then had been to help operators in modernising their fleets and, in particular, allow old types unsuitable for operation without

a conductor to be phased out more quickly.

The new bus grant was due to be phased out completely as a result of a review made by the Callaghan Government, itself under some financial pressure, in 1976-77 and it was planned gradually to reduce the grant from its level of 50 per cent of the cost of each new bus after 1980/81. This was introduced a year earlier than expected by the Thatcher Government, meaning that the grant would drop by 10 per cent per year in the period up to 1984. The pressure to get new buses built, already evident as soon as the ending of the grant was signalled, was intensified.

Demand for new double-deckers was strong, both from urban fleets and the nationalised companies, and the phasing-out of new bus grant accentuated the upsurge temporarily as operators sought to get as many of their new vehicle needs delivered in time to minimise the loss of grant. The MCW Metrobus was a remarkable success, going into production in 1978, and attracting interest from the PTEs and London Transport in particular. It was hardly surprising that

West Midlands PTE favoured the local product, and by the time the vehicle shown, 2497, had entered service in 1982 there were over 500, including prototypes, in that fleet, mostly with Gardner 6LXB engines and air-pressure brakes. Some 196 were delivered to WMPTE in 1982 alone, mostly of the newly-introduced Mark II type with simplified body construction and square-cut frontal profile lacking the asymetric windscreen of the previous version, as shown.

Overall, the demand for bus services was continuing to fall – the decline had been evident since the 'fifties as car ownership became more and more common. It followed that there was an underlying drop in demand for new buses, yet the actual picture was apt to be more complex. To some degree, operators tended to think in terms of replacing existing vehicles when this became due or desirable. For historic reasons, most fleets were far from uniform in their age profile, as the proportion of vehicles of different ages in the fleet was called. Such factors as the 1939-45 war, the massive fleet replacements that followed, replacement of tram and, later, trolleybus systems had all produced peaks and troughs in vehicle intake, quite apart from temporary pressures on finances and delays in delivery due to a variety of factors.

Another factor that was having an effect, especially in the NBC subsidiaries and to some extent in other fleets, was the effect of revised services designed to produce route networks that could be maintained from fare revenue at commercially acceptable levels. The name Market Analysis Project (MAP) was applied to these schemes, which involved considerable revision of services. A common factor that emerged was the economic benefit that resulted from wider use of double-deckers. A general tendency for NBC fleets to buy more single-deckers in the 'seventies was reversed towards the end of that decade.

The net result was that, nationally, new double-deckers were being placed in service at a rate greater than at any time since the early 'sixties. Single-deck bus deliveries were a little down, though not yet to an alarming degree, while the coach sector, unaffected by new bus grant, was still quite healthy and, overall, delivery of new vehicles to the industry was continuing at the level of about 5,500 per annum which had applied in the late 'seventies, rather higher than in the middle of that decade.

So in this sense, it could be said that there was an air of reasonable prosperity, with more than enough new vehicles to keep fleets up-to-date on a 15-year life basis if not quite enough overall for the twelve year life favoured in some concerns. To some degree, this was

misleading, for the industry was still coping with the effects of severe inflation, particularly savage in its effect on a business where fares could only be increased when it could be shown costs had already gone up. There was also the effect, familiar to almost all operators for the last 40 years or so, of falling numbers of passengers. Levels of service were reduced, inevitably with a time lag, and this itself made the services less attractive.

Inflation was coming under control, but the new Government's strict monetary policy had its cost in terms of unemployment, which began to rise rapidly, especially in manufacturing industry, though it is fair to recall also that the sharp rise in world oil prices in 1979 had also had its effect in slowing down trade generally. Fewer people travelling to and from work meant more cuts in fare revenue and in some cases wholesale changes in the pattern of services were needed because of permanent factory closures or reductions in staff.

Chapter two:
A political time-bomb

By the beginning of 1980, it was clear that the direction of political action was being reversed from what had been accepted not only in the 'seventies but in many ways a great deal longer. The climate has since altered so radically that it is difficult to understand how permanent the legislative structure as it stood up to then seemed.

This was partly because there had been a greater degree of political consensus between the two major political parties than either of them would have been willing to admit. The Labour Party had tended to increase the extent of one form of public ownership of transport facilities or another, notably in the Transport Acts of 1947 and 1968, but the Conservative Party had not seriously attempted to reverse the provisions of those Acts in more than marginal ways – until 1980.

Indeed the pattern goes back much further. The Tramways Act of 1870, when Gladstone was Prime Minister of a Liberal Government, had included provision which gave the right to municipalities to purchase tramway systems within their areas after a period of 21 years. In consequence, many city or borough councils took over the ex-company tramways operating on their streets from around the turn of the century – very often, they then substantially upgraded the networks thus acquired. Technological development was a feature of this – electrification of tramways often followed, that of the complete Leeds system, when the Corporation took over in 1894, was put into effect in 1897-1902, for example; though the first overhead-wire electric tram system in Europe had begun to operate in that same city in 1891, it had remained an isolated single-route venture.

In a similar way, municipal motor bus fleets had grown, at first usually as an adjunct to trams to cover outlying areas but eventually taking over from the trams, sometimes with trolleybuses as an intermediate stage. Here again, advanced technology was often a feature – the diesel motor bus was taken up with enthusiasm in quite a number of municipal fleets, perhaps most notably Manchester, several years before the major English company groups took it seriously, for example.

Even before the development of tramways, horse-bus operation in urban areas had led to the development of forms of control to limit what were seen very early on as the excesses of unregulated competition. It is interesting to note that only a little over two years after Shillibeer introduced his service in London in July 1829 which introduced the word omnibus to the English language, an agreement had been reached between the numerous operators by then running on the Paddington-Bank route, taking 33 buses of the 90 by then on the road out of service and introducing a three-minute frequency throughout the day from 8am to 10pm, with inspectors appointed by the operators' association which had been formed to enforce timekeeping.

No doubt some would see this as an undesirable form of cartel intended to benefit the horse-bus owners, as doubtless it was, yet the operation of a regular service with what would nowadays be regarded as a frequent headway and also reducing traffic congestion clearly had its benefits for the public.

Later, the police became involved in the regulation of services and in

The Tramways Act of 1870 provided the foundation for the widespread municipal ownership of urban tramway systems in Britain and hence the bus fleets that succeeded them in almost all cases. The sole mainland survivor is the Blackpool system, where No. 40, one of that undertaking's 'standard' cars built in the Corporation's own workshops in the 'twenties and restored at the National Tramway Museum, Crich, to near-original condition, is seen in the depot in September 1985. It is in company with Sheffield City Transport 513, one of that city's final batch of trams built to SCT design by Charles Roberts & Co, preserved after withdrawal when the Sheffield system closed in 1960 and one of a number of cars 'visiting' Blackpool in recent years.

In 1983, West Yorkshire PTE marked the centenary of the foundation of municipal tramway operation in Huddersfield, which had been noteworthy as the first known instance of direct ownership of a public transport undertaking by a local authority, in Britain at any rate. In later years, trolleybuses and motor buses replaced the trams and the Huddersfield undertaking was one of those absorbed by West Yorkshire PTE when it came into operation in April 1974. The PTE had started a new numbering series at 6001 for Leyland Atlantean AN68 models with Roe bodywork as one of its main standard types and 6299, one of 75 with PUA ...W registration numbers, was selected for painting in a version of Huddersfield's final livery.

Another notable anniversary was the 50th of the Green Line network of services, established in July 1930 as Green Line Coaches Ltd, a subsidiary of the London General Omnibus Co Ltd. From July 1933, it became part of the newly-formed London Passenger Transport Board, but the name, livery and distinctive vehicles continued and this remained so after January 1970 when it became part of London Country Bus Services Ltd, the company formed by the National Bus Company to run the ex-London Transport services based in the area outside the Greater London Council boundary. It is intriguing to note that the original Green Line management rushed to get more routes established by 9th February 1931, the last date on which new services could be started without a road service licence under the provision of the Road Traffic Act, a procedure which had continued virtually unaltered until the Transport Act 1980 began to re-open the door to direct competition. Seen bearing appropriate lettering is RS137, one of the final batch of AEC Reliance coaches with Plaxton Supreme IV bodywork purchased for Green Line duty.

many towns, quite clear-cut licensing systems were in use to control the frequency of services 100 years or more ago. As municipal electric tram services developed, the councils understandably used their powers to limit competition from motor buses of other operators, in some cases causing operators to run from private premises and forbidding them to carry passengers on journeys within the municipal area. This was clearly a restriction on passengers' freedom of action, yet it, and the milder limitations used later, also avoided the longer-distance services being swamped by local passengers.

Motor bus competition became intense in the years after the 1914-18 war, and practices such as timing services to run just in front of a competitor, what amounted to racing between stops and other forms of aggressive driving led to a view that some form of regulation on a nation-wide rather than merely local basis was desirable. The result was the Road Traffic Act of 1930, and in particular its provisions on road service licensing and the consequences mentioned in the previous chapter.

That Act was passed by a Labour Government, yet its principles and provisions relating to road service licensing of bus and coach operation were to remain virtually unchanged by successive administrations, more often Conservative or coalitions under Conservative leadership than Labour,

for virtually half a century – the Transport Act 1980 began to nibble at the principles, especially for long-distance services, but left much of the structure still operational and it was not until the Transport Act 1985 that the ideas that had been developed gradually in broadly the same direction for 160 years were almost completely abandoned.

The London story had often differed – tramway development had been kept out of central London in a way quite unlike that which occurred in the other major cities in Britain, thus fostering bus service development, both horse and then motor, to a much greater degree. In fact the motor bus, as a means of city transport, tended to be very much London-orientated for the first quarter of the 20th century, even though some of the earliest motor bus services sprang up in some remarkably remote places and were to be found in many parts of the country by 1910, though development was still very patchy.

The pattern of development in London was also very different in that company or independent operation of buses remained dominant – some of the outer boroughs had small municipal tramway systems and the London County Council built up the country's largest tram fleet, despite being virtually excluded from the centre, but none of these had moved into bus operation. The almost inevitable result was the

gradual build-up of a near-monopoly, culminating in the acquisition in 1912 of the London General Omnibus Co Ltd, by far the largest bus operator, by the Underground group which already owned almost the whole tube and electric suburban railway network except for that south of the Thames.

There were still numerous independent bus operators, though their combined fleets were much smaller and attempts were made to extend regulation, notably by the London Traffic Act of 1924, but in practice the overall picture did not alter until July 1933 when the newly-formed London Passenger Transport Board took over the Underground group's operations and set about the compulsory acquisition of independent and other operators' services within its area, which extended far beyond the urban limits of London.

Here again, the legislation was proposed by the 1929-31 Labour Government, the Bill being tabled in December 1930, yet it was passed – with some amendments but with the basic principle unaltered – after a Conservative Government had come into power and became law in April 1933.

In practice there was even greater continuity than might have been thought, for Lord Ashfield, who as Albert Stanley had been appointed to take charge of the Underground group in 1910, had adopted a philosophy based on the provision of a comprehensive network of bus and underground rail services as the primary aim long before the political change of structure creating London Transport was put into effect. This was another instance where the seemingly undesirable idea of a monopoly had provided a basis for technological development – the LGOC was widely regarded as a bus design leader, just as was London Transport in later years. The idea of what might be described as a 'free-standing' public body was in quite general favour at that time – the British Broadcasting Corporation was another example – and it is important to recall that this type of organisation was intended to pay its way, even though given a monopoly in its particular field, as well as providing high-quality service to the public.

Outside London, the Road Traffic Act also tended to give a degree of monopoly to established bus operators, though they often complained, with some justice, that the railway companies were allowed to cramp their freedom by the rights they had to object to any proposal for new or altered services that might threaten to draw passengers from rail services. The Traffic Commissioners were under instruction to take a serious view of what was called abstraction of traffic from established road or rail services.

The principle behind this was simply that the economics of providing a bus or train service depended on a sufficient number of passengers paying their fares. If a competing service were to be permitted, passengers would be likely to be drawn from the existing one, and it was argued that this was undesirable, since it undermined the basis on which it could be provided. As an extension of that idea, it became accepted practice – though not directly written down as a specific rule – that the major operator in an area, usually one of the area-agreement companies, would be expected to 'take the rough with the smooth'. In other words, not all routes, even in the 'thirties, could be expected to pay their way, and as an implied expectation of being permitted to earn the good profits obtainable on a major trunk service, some at least of that money should cover losses in the provision of services in more remote parts of the territory covered.

As independent bus operators tended to sell out, so the concept of network coverage by the big company grew, although the degree to which this happened varied and even in 1980 some parts of the country had quite large-scale independent operator involvement in the provision of local services. In the more remote areas, the large operators were no longer enthusiastic to buy up businesses which, if required to carry higher overheads related to the inevitably more complex organisation of a large firm, could not be profitable. Gradually, as bus revenue fell due to the wider use of cars and in the aftermath of the Transport Act of 1968 and the

Local Government Act of 1972, the idea of county council support for services grew, at first in such deep rural areas but later covering a broader spectrum of routes which, for one reason or another, were important to local communities but could not directly pay.

I have included this potted history to convey how the senior bus managers of 1980, largely men in their 'fifties or older, had not only a lifetime's involvement with the route licensing system as it had stood since the 1930 Act, but whose predecessors had also operated within a similar framework. When Norman Fowler, shadow spokesman on transport when the Conservative Party had been in opposition in the period before 1979 and a close ally of Margaret Thatcher throughout his career, had begun to speak of more radical changes the full implications seem to have been dismissed by senior members of the operating industry. They had heard politicians with extreme-sounding views, either of the left or right, before and yet when they had come to office, the realities had tempered such views down to much nearer the general consensus.

But this time it was different. The 1980 Act gave a taste of what was to follow in relation to the longer-distance coach services. Doubtless they had come to mind as being an easier problem to tackle, both in the sense of operational complexity and also in that many independent operators had expressed a

The principle of network provision of services, and with it an element of cross-subsidy from busy urban services to those in country areas, tended to grow under the road service licence system created as a result of the Road Traffic Act 1930. United Automobile Services Ltd was an example of an operator with a very varied mix of services in its extensive area stretching from the Scottish border at Berwick as far south as Ripon in Yorkshire. During the 'seventies a substantial fleet of Bristol LH buses with ECW bodywork, generally seating 45 passengers, had been built up for rural services, No. 1602, seen here in Hexham on the Allendale service in June 1983, being typical.

The Scottish Bus Group's network included many routes serving remote areas. Highland Omnibuses L51, a Leyland Leopard with Alexander Y-type bus body, pulls into a passing place on a narrow road on the Isle of Skye in July 1985. Despite the absence of big centres of population, such services could sometimes carry heavy traffic in the tourist season and it is noteworthy that the vehicle shown was one of a number of Leopards in the Highland fleet with seats for 62 passengers — it had originally been operated by Alexander (Fife) but was transferred to Highland in 1983.

wish for greater freedom of action. Scheduled services linking most towns and cities were very largely in the hands of the State-owned NBC or SBG subsidiaries, though there were a handful of independent operators – most notably Grey Green in London, Premier Travel of Cambridge and Yelloway of Rochdale – who had become recognised and operated jointly with the major companies, having access to their coach stations. In addition, there were many independents who ran holiday-related services of a regular though largely seasonal nature.

Long-distance coach travel had long had its own clientele, among whom both the elderly and young figured quite largely – and to whom its combination of low fares and, generally, slower schedules than offered by trains were acceptable. It was widely recognised that, on some routes at least, such business could be built up, but the licensing procedures and, in particular railway opposition, had caused it to be restricted – for example, there were often severe limits on the amount of duplication of popular timings that were allowed.

It was doubtless felt that this would also be a useful dry run for the wider changes which were proposed. Certainly there was a view quite widely held in 1980 that the independents, given their freedom, would make

Motorways had greatly increased the potential for coaches to compete with railways, especially where the comparison of available routes was favourable. Here a Midland Red Leyland Leopard coach with Plaxton Panorama Elite body in NBC white coach livery heads for Bristol on the M5 in the mid-'seventies. The NBC express coach network was to prove more effective than the more doctrinaire members of the Government expected when coach deregulation exposed it to direct competition.

Quite a number of independent operators were keen to expand their long-distance services. Park's of Hamilton was one of those which chose imported coaches of advanced mechanical design for long-distance duty, among which the MAN SR280 was notable, with integral construction, rear-mounted 280bhp engine and independent front suspension. Park's JLS 2V is seen at the rather bleak King's Cross terminal used by independent operators in November 1981. By that date, Park's had been operating to London for a little over a year as a member of the British Coachways consortium, but it was not proving the success its founders had hoped, as described in the next chapter.

serious inroads into the NBC/SBG near-monopoly. Some of the more doctrinaire believers in the merits of private enterprise and unrestricted competition thought that the exercise would demonstrate the superiority of their beliefs with something approaching the collapse of the nationalised sector in this field, providing a useful prelude to what was to follow and in gaining public acceptance for the principles.

The most prominent provision of the Transport Act 1980 was the deregulation of services with a minimum passenger journey length of 30 miles (often summarised as 'coach deregulation'). This created a situation which was quite revolutionary within this field, for not only did it roll back what had existed since the 1930 legislation but went further, since even in the 'twenties many local authorities had exercised quite tight control within their areas as indicated above and this affected long-distance as well as local services. Moreover, the existence of the motorway network and the greatly improved performance of modern

vehicles meant that some scheduled journey times could be more competitive with rail than in those days – subject to traffic delay, of course.

Less publicised, though significant as pointers to what was to follow, were the removal of the Traffic Commissioners' powers in relation to fares, though this drastic change was tempered by the wording 'except where essential to regulate competition between stage carriage services or to protect the public from abuse of monopoly powers'. Had the situation continued for long, the exact meaning of these rather vague phrases might well have been subject to legal challenge, but the real point was perhaps to indicate that the old order of tight control of fares was under notice.

A third significant change was the introduction of a presumption in favour of an applicant for a road service licence. One of the complaints of independent operators of the road service licensing system since 1930 was that there was an in-built bias the opposite way, making it rather like an exclusive club

in which the established operators resisted the appearance of any newcomer. Here again, the effect was perhaps one of signalling a change in climate and attitude. A few newcomers did appear on the scene, and perhaps more significantly, the provision for allowing what was intended to be a try-out of the new era in local services in the so-called 'trial areas', where deregulation of bus services would be permitted within specified boundaries, was exercised though in rural districts which gave no clue to the behaviour to be expected in urban areas.

The real changes in local services were to be embodied in the Transport Act 1985, the campaign towards which, together with other consequences of political action, will be examined in later chapters.

In a more general way, the typical local transport scene of the early 'eighties showed little sign of the major changes that were coming. A mixture of area-agreement company and independent vehicles was to be seen parked at the traditional site at The Strand, Dumfries, on the banks of the River Nith, in September 1983, much as they had for over half a century. A Ford R1114 with Duple Dominant body of Gibson's of Moffat on the service from that town waits alongside a Western SMT Seddon Pennine VII with Alexander T-type body bound for Glasgow.

The National Express fleetname first appeared at the end of 1980 in the wake of coach deregulation – previously NBC coaches in the white livery adopted as a corporate standard in 1972 had carried the single word National with alternate letters in red and blue. It was to be the sole part of the identity to be sold off when privatised and survives today on the vehicles hired by National Express Ltd.

Here a Leyland Leopard with Plaxton Supreme IV 57-seat bodywork, No. 355 in the fleet of National Travel (South West) Ltd, shows off the then new style on its introduction. The vehicle was of 12-metre length, by then increasingly popular, the chassis being of the PSU5D/4R type.

Chapter Three:
Coach deregulation arrives

The intention of Mrs Thatcher's Government to adopt a philosophy based on the encouragement of competition became evident soon after it took office in May 1979, even if the extent to which this would be taken was not clear at that stage. In particular, so far as the bus and coach industry was concerned, there was the Transport Bill introduced later that year, with its intention to deregulate coach services and begin slackening the knot of road service licensing which largely held together the structure of the industry as it stood.

Well before the Bill became an Act on 30th June 1980, the industry was buzzing with speculation. It was hardly surprising that the coaching symposium

held by the Coach and Independent Bus Sector of what was then called CPT (the Confederation of British Road Passenger Transport) held in March 1980 concentrated on the subject, with a paper by Ron Whittle of J. T. Whittle & Son of Highley, Shropshire, widely recognised as one of the livelier independent operators. He drew attention not only to the opportunities for new services but also the dangers, fearing a price war leading to bankruptcy for the unwary.

However, active planning on how best to succeed in the new climate was engaging the attention of the more far-seeing management teams. Ironically, it may well have been true that the depth of such studies was nowhere

greater than within the State-owned National Bus Company, despite the fact that the new 'received wisdom' was that nationalised industry was inherently inefficient.

At first attention was largely concentrated on coach operation in view of the known intention to deregulate services of this character in the autumn of 1980, the precise date being set as 6th October of that year. NBC had gone through a series of reorganisations of its coach-operating activities beginning in 1972, though outside observers – such as politicians – might have been forgiven for thinking that these had been only partially effective and hence that its prospects in a competitive environment were not very good. One

There had been a growing 'commercial' approach to express coach operation in particular during the late 'seventies, but the deregulation of such services on 6th October 1980 brought new examples of the hard sell. Here National Travel (West) No. 1256, a 12-metre Leyland Leopard with Duple Dominant II 53-seat bodywork is seen two days before the event bearing lettering extolling both the time and airline-style low standby fare for the Liverpool-Manchester service. There had been repeated reorganisations of NBC express service operation in the north west of England – National Travel (North West) Ltd had been set up in 1974, being actually the old North Western Road Car Co Ltd renamed, taking over North Western and Ribble services and coaches, being renamed again in a further re-jig as National Travel (West), but in 1984 the wheel was almost to turn full circle as Ribble then took over National Travel (West)'s northern operations, including this vehicle.

of the problems was the inherent tug-of-war between the concept of a uniform centrally-planned network along the lines of the Greyhound system in the United States, as introduced here soon after his appointment as NBC Chairman by Freddie (later Sir Frederick) Wood, and the practical fact that most of the group's coaches were owned and run by subsidiaries whose main business was running local bus services.

Gradually, ways of overcoming those problems were found, and it is a curious fact that the one part of NBC as a national organisation that still exists in recognisable form in 1991 is National Express, a title adopted as fleetname in the aftermath of deregulation at the end of 1980, taken up as a company title in 1981 and developed into a trading concern in May 1984 in the run-up to the bigger changes embodied in the Transport Act 1985. The organisation was built up on the basis that it did not itself own vehicles and this continued through the process of privatisation – when sold off to a management team in March 1988 some 950 coaches were operated on a contract basis but only four were owned by National Express itself. The company took over the sole right to use of the NBC logo and continues to use the same style of fleetname lettering as introduced at the end of 1980.

In fact, although most express services as running in early 1980 were recognisably derived from the network

existing not only before 1972 but very largely that of the 'thirties (including the Associated Motorways and other joint-service networks), there was a distinct sharpening up within NBC's coach operation, nicely in time for the new regime of October 1980 onwards. Some of this had begun before there was any sign of the political upheaval of 1979, for the Market Analysis Project (MAP) techniques of analysing actual and potential traffic originally developed for bus services by NBC staff were adapted to coach operation from the winter of 1978/79. The data thus obtained was used in the formulation of a new winter timetable brought into effect on 21st September 1980, just before deregulation came came into effect on 6th October.

The lifting of operating restrictions made it possible to timetable more departures, with reduced journey times and the need to be able to alter services to deal with competition or react to changing demand was indicated in what might seem a minor detail, though a significant one – the adoption of loose-leaf timetable and faretable books.

The independent operators most interested in express service operation had not been idle, meanwhile. The strength of the NBC in terms of a nationwide network was recognised – extending into Scotland if Scottish Bus Group services were also taken into account, they being similarly developed to take advantage of the new

circumstances. The answer was the formation of a consortium, given the title British Coachways to give a similarly 'nationwide' image. Rather cheekily, the style of lettering was similar to that used by British Airways at the time, but with 'coach' emphasised by the use of blue lettering to contrast with the remainder in red. The extent of Government encouragement is conveyed by the presence at the opening of services of no less than the Secretary of State for Transport, Norman Fowler.

The original participants were Wallace Arnold Tours Ltd of Leeds (then operating about 290 coaches); Ellerman Bee Line Ltd, based in Middlesbrough (70 coaches); Grey-Green Coaches Ltd, London (100 coaches); Morris Bros of Swansea Ltd (50 coaches); Park's of Hamilton (60 coaches), and Shearings Holidays Ltd of Altrincham, part of the Shearings Group (with a total of 138 coaches). A small number of coaches were painted in British Coachways livery, somewhat similar to National white but with more extensive red and blue relief, though individual operators' interpretations varied slightly.

From deregulation day, 6th October 1980, services connecting London with Middlesbrough and Newcastle; Sheffield, Leeds and Bradford; Birmingham, Liverpool/Manchester and Glasgow; Cardiff and Swansea, and Bristol. Plymouth/Torbay were operated. Fares were very low – £4

single from London to Liverpool, for example, which undercut even the £9 standby return introduced by National Express, the latter's normal return being £13.20 to £18.50 depending on the day of travel. However, National cut its fares on competing services to match those of British Coachways.

Inevitably, margins were very low, and it is hardly surprising that the membership of the consortium did not remain stable for long. By the summer of 1981 Wallace Arnold and Grey-Green, both key organisations in the venture, had left, for example. On the other hand, Barton Transport Ltd of Beeston, Nottingham, and Excelsior Travel Ltd joined. After the first year's operation, British Coachways were able to celebrate that 750,000 passengers had been carried, but this is put into perspective by the comparable figure for NBC express services of 12.5 million (up from 8.5 million in 1980). Grey-

This newspaper-style leaflet was issued to publicise the British Coachways venture set up by six leading independent operators in 1980 – on inside pages, it gave timetables for services linking London to Newcastle (service numbers 100-3), to Yorkshire (104-7), to Bristol and Devon (300-7), to South Wales (400-3) and to Birmingham (Liverpool/Manchester and Glasgow (500-7, 600-5) – the route numbering was on the same principle as the Ministry of Transport's scheme for road numbering. Ironically there was an unashamed affinity to the then still State-owned British Airways publicity and lettering.

Only small numbers of vehicles appeared in British Coachways livery; the participating companies retained their own styles for vehicles on other duty and few were repainted while new deliveries were apt to be split according to their intended duties. Seen here is PDC 603X, a Leyland Leopard with Plaxton Supreme IV bodywork of Ellerman Bee Line Ltd, seen while being cleaned by decidedly basic means after arriving in London from Newcastle and Middlesbrough in November 1981, not long after entering service. Unsatisfactory premises for both loading passengers and vehicle servicing was the main weakness of the British Coachways set-up. The name Ellerman had been familiar to earlier generations as that of a shipping line, but the take-over of Bee Line, an independent operator originally based in West Hartlepool, though later in Middlesbrough, as part of the Gold Case Travel Group in 1977 brought it into coaching. In later years, Bee Line was to be adopted as a fleetname by at least two quite unrelated concerns for local bus services.

Green, which had a long-standing friendly relationship with NBC, joined National Express on a new joint Romford-Birmingham service.

Although there was a new spirit of competition, relations between NBC and most of the major independents which had run express services previously were not unfriendly, and pooling arrangements with Wallace Arnold on Torbay services and Grey-Green on routes in East Anglia continued. Both Premier Travel and Yelloway, long-established partners with NBC subsidiaries, chose not to

compete, while Whittle, after a period of direct competition, entered a new agreement with NBC on services between the West Midlands and London.

London was a target for quite a number of other independent operators' new services – indeed some were new operators previously virtually unknown. A particularly revealing entry in The Omnibus *Magazine* of November/ December 1980 reviewing new services from Scotland and after a section on British Coachways reads 'The main independent effort appears to be a Mr

Although not one of the original participants, Barton Transport Ltd joined British Coachways after a few months. Here No. 572 in the Barton fleet stands in a waterlogged corner of the Kings Cross terminal site in March 1981 with a windscreen sticker bearing the name Londonliner but including the British Coachways title and Union flag. Once again the vehicle was a Plaxton-bodied Leyland Leopard, for there was wide agreement on the merits of this chassis for express duty, though in this case it was PSU3E/4R with Supreme Express 53-seat body – Barton used basically similar vehicles for many of its services and such a seating capacity on an 11-metre coach was in contrast to the growing trend towards more spacious and elaborate accommodation for passengers.

Another arrival at the depressing Kings Cross premises on the same day in March 981 was LYS 457P, a weathered-looking Volvo B58 with Duple Dominant 49-seat bodywork operated by an unknown firm with the name Gloag which adopted 'The Stage Coach' as its fleetname for a Dundee-London service which had begun immediately after deregulation in October 1980. The vehicle had quite a chequered earlier career, being one of a pair built for a Metropolitan Traffic Area operator who cancelled the order, whereupon they were purchased by Park of Hamilton in September 1975, running for a time with Cotter's fleetname, but sold to A. Wilson of Greenock in 1977. Who would have guessed that Stagecoach would become the most extensive bus company group in Britain before the end of the decade?

Gloag (t/a Stagecoach Travel) of 186 Glasgow Road, Perth, who started a Dundee-London service on 9th October ...' It operated via Perth and it was reported that Scottish Bus Group was prompted to display one of its M-type motorway coaches in Perth for a day, even though there was no SBG London service from that city. Yet in less than eight years Brian Souter and his sister Ann Gloag had become among the best known names in the industry and their Stagecoach organisation had a bought three major NBC subsidiaries.

Another opportunity recognised by a wide variety of operators was that of running commuter coach services, again with London as the main target. The stranglehold given to the railways over coach operators by the pre-1980 licensing system was particularly strong in regard to services which could be

used by people wishing to travel say 50 miles into London from the areas which, to a considerable extent, could be regarded as dormitory country. The same phenomenon was much less marked elsewhere, partly because a lower proportion of people travel by rail into provincial cities and indeed the longer-distance commuter using any form of transport is not such a common phenomenon.

Although most of the NBC subsidiaries in the area surrounding London have run coach services into Victoria Coach Station ever since it opened in 1932, their timings, in response to railway protestations in the traffic courts, were singularly unhelpful to anyone wanting to get to work in the Capital at a reasonable hour. The British Rail network was handling vast numbers of passengers of this type, as it had done

for a century or more, but complaints of high fares and overcrowding left scope for an effective alternative.

Not surprisingly, several independent operators recognised the opportunity. Heyfordian Travel Ltd introduced its Capital Express between Oxford and London, with a £2.50 day return fare and others included Gastonia from Cranleigh and Olsen from the Medway towns. A particularly interesting development, representing a complete departure from the idea that municipal undertakings should confine their activities to their own areas or, at most, that just beyond, was the joint service operated by the Reading and Southend Transport, linking those towns via London and also calling at London Airport. The service used double-deckers with seating to coach standards, Southend further breaking

The sight of a municipal bus operating on a licensed service in London was strange, as was the idea of such a vehicle operating an express service far beyond its own area. Reading Transport adopted the name Goldline for vehicles with coach seating on the service to London, originally extending through to Southend and run jointly with the latter's transport department. Number 189 was the first of a batch of five MCW Metrobuses to this specification and having Gardner engines and air-pressure brakes, placed in service in 1982 and seen in company with London Routemaster RM1219 dating from 1962, in April 1983.

In spite of its limitations, Victoria Coach Station was greatly superior as a London coach terminal to anything available to independent operators and, together with other coach stations up and down the country equally well-known in their own localities, gave NBC a strong advantage not only in facilities but also because the co-ordination of services also made it an important interchange point. In some ways, it was the victim of the success of NBC's coach network simply because it became greatly overcrowded. This view, dating from the mid-'eighties, shows how the once-tidy segregation of routes to specific departure bays appropriately identified had largely been abandoned. Even so, it was clean, dry and 'civilised' by comparison with the bleak locations from which independent operators had to run.

with tradition in using some of imported origin.

However, NBC was also not slow to exploit the possibilities, and a whole series of services was introduced, with names such as Londonlink, Invictaway, London City Link emphasising the associations at one end or the other. A Transport and Road Research Laboratory study covering the period between June 1981 and January 1983 showed that the number of coaches on such services into London operated by public sector operators, mainly NBC but also the municipal undertakings mentioned above, rose from 26 to 91. Over the same period, the figures for the private sector – in other words, independent operators, rose from 33 to 76. Further new services of this type were introduced in 1983 to 1985.

Overall, however, the attempt to challenge National Express with a rival independent network had collapsed. Shearings had taken over the responsibility of marketing for British Coachways after Wallace Arnold and Grey-Green withdrew, but it too pulled out in August 1982. The final partners – Barton, Ellerman Bee Line, Excelsior and Park's split up on 18th October 1982, the day on which the London terminal they had been using, the London Ryan Hotel in King's Cross Road, ceased to be available to them.

In fact the lack of satisfactory coach terminal points in major cities was perhaps the Achilles heel of the whole British Coachways venture. Victoria Coach Station had long had its limitations but even so provided NBC with a terminal point already well known to millions of passengers, actual or potential. It also acted as an interchange point, a survey revealing that almost 1 in 4 of passengers arriving at Victoria departed from it by other connecting coach services. The same applied to a lesser degree to such similar cases as Digbeth in Birmingham –

hardly impressive as barely more than a garage, yet in a recognised location near the city centre. The existing NBC services were known to a sizeable slice of the population in each area and the location of the coach stations they served equally well known, so new routes linking them had a major advantage over independent services rarely running to established locations. The problem of a London terminal had plagued independent operators since the 'thirties, with repeated moves between locations in the region of King's Cross, and the lack of anything suitable was particularly serious at such a time of opportunity. At first, British Coachways used the site of the former St. Pancras goods depot by then demolished and thus resembling the 'bomb site' car parks familiar in London just after the war and about as bleak. It recently came into the news again as the site of the British Library building.

Thus NBC not only repelled the

anticipated attack on its express service network but gained considerably from the 1980 coach deregulation exercise. A factor that had been forgotten was that the road service licensing system had been particularly frustrating for the managers, very knowledgeable in their field, who were responsible for many of the subsidiaries' express services, which had long had a strong following among passengers who found them better suited to their needs than rail services, but were artificially restricted by conditions imposed on the licenses. It was a little like a coiled spring suddenly released, aided by the MAP-based study which came at a particularly opportune time.

There had been strong pressure to improve the performance of NBC's coach operations as a whole, seen as more potentially profitable than bus services, long suffering from declining numbers of passengers and rising costs. A specialised coach holiday unit had been formed in 1977, after a disastrous period when airline competition cut into the Continental holidays business so severely that sale of all the relevant licences to Bee Line of Middlesbrough

was seriously considered. It was based in Sheffield – an appropriate location in view of the strong tradition of Sheffield United Tours in this field until it vanished in the early 'seventies when NBC decided to abandon such identities at the height of the NBC corporate identity drive. The SUT company, dormant since 1974, was renamed National Holidays Ltd in 1980 and although this company did not begin trading as a separate entity until 1984, the fleetname was applied to coaches used on such duties from 1981. A better understanding of the changing needs of potential users and, it has to be said, a shift from the concept of a coach tour operator to a holiday company had turned the business round. By 1985, some 3,300,000 passengers per year were being carried compared to 100,000 on the equivalent operations ten years earlier.

Just how much the coach activities of NBC contributed to its earnings was a subject which had at least a tinge of controversy. The problem was how to disentangle the costs of the coach activities from those of the bus businesses which were the main activity

of the group as a whole. Clearly the vehicles and the direct running costs could be readily identified. Staff costs were a little more complex as some of the drivers worked on both bus and coach duties – a logical situation, since express service demand tended to be higher at weekends when bus duties were fewer than during the working week for the population as a whole, but one which complicated separate accounting. Similarly, garaging maintenance and overhaul was generally carried out in premises and by staff mainly used for buses.

NBC quoted a contribution to overall profitability of £3.1 million from National Express and £0.9 million for National Holidays for 1980, a year when NBC as a whole made an overall loss of £11.8 million, largely due to the recession, which caused a sharp drop in numbers of passengers carried on bus services. The figures for that year were affected by the onset of coach deregulation from October as well as the revised National Express services, but the resulting rise in earnings, despite the period of intense competition with British Coachways, was reflected in an

National Holidays began to be used as a fleetname for NBC coaches engaged on appropriate duties from 1981. The vehicles were owned by existing subsidiaries and this view shows two of a fleet of ten Bova 52-seat coaches of the EL26/581 type of National Travel (London) Ltd, the successor to National Travel (South East) Ltd, for the 1982 season. The Bova, with DAF engine and axles, was building up a sizeable following in Britain and the securing of orders

from NBC subsidiaries was significant, for there had been resistance to the purchase of imported vehicles by a State-owned organisation. However, the model was competitive in price with conventional British coaches despite the combination of integral construction, rear-engined layout and quite an advanced specification, increasingly important in a competitive market.

increase in National Express working profits to £3.9 million in 1981. The corresponding National Holidays figure was £558,000.

One senses a certain disbelief at these results in Government circles. The Secretary of State for Transport asked that the results be restated on what was described as a full allocation of costs to the three activities; stage-carriage (bus) operation, National Express and National Holidays. In *National Bus Company – a commemorative volume*, published by TPC and compiled by a team led by John A. Birks, who was Chief Executive Officer of National Express in 1979-84, the allocation is described as 'arbitrary'. On this, clearly much harsher, basis, the National Express working profit was cut back to £318,000 and National Holidays made a working loss of £32,000. However, passengers carried continued to rise, reaching 14 million in 1982 and the profit on this

same 'fully allocated costs' basis became £1.6 million; on NBC's existing basis the contribution to profit was £6 million. In a similar way, National Holidays climbed, making a contribution of £714,000 in 1983; on the full cost basis this scaled down to a small surplus of £14,000. Clearly figures of this kind were open to debate, but it is significant that National Holidays was the first NBC company to be privatised, a management offer being outbid by one from Pleasurama Ltd, the sale taking place on 14th July 1986. National Express was one of the last, going to a management team on 17th March 1988, but its survival in essentially unchanged form at the time of writing conveys durability in difficult times.

It would be quite wrong to give the impression that all the activity was within NBC, even though its dominance in express service working was one of the key elements of the early 'eighties.

Some independent operators were important innovators, and among them were some who pioneered the use of vehicles of more advanced design. Generally, the British Coachways members used typical 'standard' coaches of that era, the Shearings contribution to vehicles painted in the consortium livery being two Ford R1114 models with Plaxton bodywork, for example, though on the whole heavier-duty chassis such as Leyland Leopard or the Volvo B58 coming into increasing favour with independent operators were more often favoured. However, Park's used MAN SR280 rear-engined models and the greater standard of comfort was clearly of importance on a route as long as the Glasgow-London run.

In rather a similar way, F. G. Trathen & Son of Yelverton, Devon, a coach operator previously little known outside that area, caught the headlines with its Plymouth-London service using the

One of the independent operators which helped to pioneer the concept of using high-specification coaches was Cotter Tours Ltd of Glasgow, which began a service to London in December 1980 using four new Volvo coaches with Van Hool Alizée bodywork and W-suffix registrations. They were fitted with toilet and galley facilities as well as reclining seats for 40 passengers, and hostess service was provided. Each vehicle cost £75,000, about 50 per cent more than a good-quality 'standard' coach of the period. Further similar vehicles were added to the fleet but in 1983 it was decided to re-register them to eliminate the 'dating' effect of the registration suffix letters, a growing trend among coach operators at that time, and when this publicity photograph was taken in Aberdeen the two of them shown had become LJC 800 and ORY 640. The Cotter concern went into receivership in 1987, its activities being taken over by Wallace Arnold.

Among the key names in the reshaping of the coach operating industry in the early 'eighties, that of F. G. Trathen & Son was outstanding. Prior to 1980, it was barely known outside the area around the village of Yelverton in Devon, though as this is about eight miles north of Plymouth, there was a good local catchment area for the Continental tours it operated. However, the new freedom was exploited and Trathens (the possessive apostrophe was dropped in the fleetname) not only began running an express service from Plymouth to London but acquired a succession of exotic vehicles for the purpose. Most dramatic of all was the purchase of two Neoplan Skyliner six-wheel double-deck coaches placed in service in November 1981 when the route, which had been run for over a year, became a joint operation with National Express, although at first the National Express workings were sub-contracted back to Trathens. The name Rapide was applied, though not with the prominence used by National Express on a wider scale later. The Skyliner had been a familiar sight in its native Germany and elsewhere since 1968, but these were the first two to enter service in Britain and indeed, although there had been earlier double-deck coaches, the progenitors of a new breed of such vehicles in this country. They seated 70, of which 52 were on the upper deck, and had Mercedes-Benz ten-cylinder vee-form engines – STT 601X is seen at the Gloucester Road, London, terminus.

The idea of providing a combination of high speed and improved interior comfort, with hostess service of light refreshments, a toilet and video facilities was taken up in a big way by National Express, using the Rapide name. During 1982, such services were introduced on additional routes, radiating from London to Swansea, Manchester, Leeds and Newcastle, some using hired vehicles in agreement with independent operators, though the development of suitable coaches for use by NBC subsidiaries was pursued urgently.

M5 and M4 motorways and operated with vehicles of more advanced specification and with hostess service for refreshments. Various makes of coach were used – the firm had standardised on Volvo chassis from the late 'seventies but in 1981 two of the Neoplan six-wheel double-deck coaches were introduced and the fleet also included MAN and Mercedes-Benz rear-engined single-deck coaches. After the service had been running a little more than a year a deal was reached with National Express under which the service was brought under the National Express umbrella, though still operated by Trathens, using the Rapide name to identify the higher-grade level of service. A similar deal was reached with Wallace Arnold.

National Express then began to introduce its own Rapide vehicles for a much broader extension of the idea, at first using conventional Leyland coaches, but subsequently a fleet of ten specially-designed Dennis Falcon V coaches with rear-mounted Perkins V8 engines, Voith automatic transmission and Duple bodywork were placed in service in the latter part of 1982. They were impressive performers but had been designed and built very quickly, so it was not too surprising that some defects affecting reliability became evident.

Meanwhile MCW had been developing its six-wheel double-deck coach design, the Metroliner, introduced at the Motor Show at the National Exhibition Centre, Birmingham, in October 1982. This vehicle was for the Scottish Bus Group and was placed in service on the Glasgow-London route in April 1983 but the announcement of an order for

Although there had been radical changes in many aspects of the coach industry, it would be wrong to suggest that either operation or rolling stock had altered out of recognition. This scene in May 1984, with a Leyland coach of Wallace Arnold Tours Ltd of Leeds, visiting Hawes en route to or from a Lake District tour could have been reproduced, with appropriate change of vehicle model, at any time in the previous half century, except for the war years. The Leyland Leopard had been strongly favoured from soon after its introduction, in 30ft. form, in 1959 though most of the fleet were 11-metre (36ft.) versions, and Plaxton bodywork had accounted for a major share of Wallace Arnold's needs since the mid-'fifties. The vehicle shown, PNW 332W, one of 20 Leopards of the PSU3F/4 type delivered in 1981, that season's intake also including ten 12-metre Leopards and fifteen Ford R1114, all with Plaxton bodywork, but imported makes began to figure more prominently in later years.

39 for National Express later that year was quite dramatic. Of these, sixteen were to be to Rapide specification with toilet and refreshment facilities and the rest to Express standard, without these features. Further orders for both NBC and SBG followed and a smaller but significant contract was for four for Tyne & Wear PTE for use on its new Clipper non-stop London-Newcastle service in July 1984, using its Armstrong Galley coaching fleetname. The subject of coach vehicle types is examined

more deeply in Chapter Seven.

Overall, coach deregulation was widely welcomed by operators of almost all types. The services requiring a road service licence that were affected by the withdrawal of the licensing system were able to reach their 'natural' potential – often very much expanded in relation to the routes between cities and the larger towns, even if some of the more outlying places lost in terms of frequency or even provision of a service at all. The dropping of the

network approach (except, ironically, by National Express itself, where it lives on to a considerable extent as a benign 'ghost' of NBC as a whole) was not so dramatic in overall effect as might have been anticipated or was to be found later with bus deregulation, partly because coach journeys tend to be pre-planned to a greater degree and people are prepared to have to make enquiries as to what is available.

The growth in demand for long-distance travel by coach resulting from the lifting of the restrictions, in particular those imposed as a result of railway pressure, of the old licensing system, pointed up the need for large-capacity vehicles. The MCW Metroliner met that demand without the limitations on internal headroom of imported vehicles built to suit Continental 4-metre overall height requirements. One of the Eastern Scottish batch of three Metroliners built in 1984 is seen at Buchanan bus station, Glasgow, on an Edinburgh-Glasgow airport service, though primarily intended for the London service.

The approval, after appeal, by the Secretary of State for Transport, Norman Fowler, of an application to run a pair of circular services in Whitehaven in competition with existing services provided by the local NBC subsidiary, Cumberland Motor Services Ltd, caused shocked surprise in the operating industry, as it appeared to run counter to the law as it was then generally understood. Yeowart's began operation in October 1981 and among its yellow-painted vehicles was this Leyland Leopard with Fowler (no relation) bodywork formerly owned by J. Fishwick & Sons of Leyland – the display in the windscreen includes reference to fares of 20p for adults and 15p for children and old-age pensioners.

Chapter Four:
Signs of change for bus services

The Transport Act 1980 made little immediate impact on stage carriage operation, then still the official designation for what are generally called bus services. The wording of the clause removing the Traffic Commissioners' powers in relation to fares with its qualification 'except where essential to regulate competition' still had enough of the familiar approach to inhibit much action of a competitive kind, and undoubtedly traffic managers were probably more relieved not to have to go through the elaborate procedure for an increase in fares related to inflation than anything else.

The introduction of the principle of presumption in favour of an applicant for a road service licence might have been expected to stir up a crop of fresh applications from independent operators wishing to get into bus operation, but this did not happen on any large scale at that stage. On the whole, there was a general feeling that buses did not make money whereas coaches were more likely to prove profitable. In the more rural areas the problem had more often become one of

finding an operator willing to provide a service, and the county councils were coming under increasing pressure to keep their outgoings in check. On more promising territory, few concerns considered challenging the major operators on their own ground, especially at a time when the recession was causing the latter to cut existing services, in some cases quite drastically.

An exception to this occurred in Whitehaven, where a small local operator, Yeowart's Coaches, applied to operate a pair of circular town routes using roads almost entirely already served by the NBC subsidiary Cumberland Motor Services Ltd, the newcomer running only at times of peak demand, with no early or late workings and no Sunday service. Cumberland objected, this action being supported by Cumbria County Council, and Yeowart's application was refused by the Northern Area Traffic Commissioners. The application went to appeal and the Inspector appointed to advise on this recommended confirmation of the refusal, but the Secretary of State for Transport decided

to allow the appeal.

This decision caused considerable consternation in the industry, to which it was a sharp lesson of how the climate in which operators worked was changing. Yeowart's services began on 19th October 1981, with fares below those charged by Cumberland. The latter responded by revising its town services to provide a circular facility, introducing the sales name 'Haven Link'. Even so, there was a loss of revenue which led directly to the withdrawal of several rural services which had been cross-subsidised by the Whitehaven town services and the loss of employment for fifteen members of staff. The yellow-painted Yeowart vehicles included two Leyland Leopard buses with Fowler bodywork originally operated by Fishwick of Leyland and a Leyland National was also purchased, much to Cumberland's annoyance, that model being built nearby as a joint Leyland and NBC venture, Cumberland having been the first operator of the type.

Another instance of independent operator incursion into types of service generally the preserve of major operators was that involving CK Coaches, which began operating various second-hand double-deckers on routes competing with Cardiff Corporation services during 1982.

There was also considerable concern inside the industry regarding the 'trial areas', within which the need for road service licences were to be lifted for a period of two years, the aim being to provide a basis for deciding whether such a policy could be applied generally. Three areas were chosen, in Norfolk, Devon and Herefordshire, and with hindsight the omission of anything approaching a major urban or industrial area is striking. At the time, there was strong opposition from major operators to such trials, for, as indicated above in the Whitehaven case, the assumptions made struck at the whole principle of cross-subsidy, on which much of the structure of both NBC and SBG was based. The initiative as to which areas should be chosen came from county councils which volunteered. It followed that they were likely to be ones that were sympathetic, so it was hardly surprising that they were the type of area of similar political view to the Government as well as lacking direct experience of running a bus undertaking.

The first came into effect on 5th April 1981, covering much of western Norfolk, almost entirely rural except for a small part of Norwich, insufficient in itself to promote a test of competitive working in the outskirts of that city.

The National Bus Company management took the Yeowart's case very seriously. Robert Brook, the group's Chief Executive, visited the Cumberland company when the Haven Link service had been devised in response and is seen facing the camera standing on the entrance step of a suitably lettered Leyland National. On the pavement alongside him is Peter Townley, Cumberland's General Manager. The early and mid-'eighties were to be difficult years for Robert Brook as NBC came under increasing pressure from a Government fundamentally opposed to State-owned enterprises and many of the concepts on which he had sought to develop the organisation.

Whatever expectations the politicians, local and national, had, in practice nothing significant happened, and the same was also true of east Devon.

The Herefordshire experiment was different, and although at the time barely taken seriously by almost all sectors of the operating industry which rejected the reasoning as faulty, to say the least, it was to prove important as a prototype for what was to follow. Some background factors are significant and I am indebted to an article by C. S. Dunbar, who is immensely knowledgeable about transport in that area, in the October 1984 issue of *Buses* for drawing attention to some of them. In the 1974 reorganisation of local government, Herefordshire and Worcestershire were amalgamated to become the county of Hereford and Worcester. There was a strong Conservative majority in the new authority – Herefordshire had been more evenly balanced and in Charles Dunbar's view would not have pursued the idea of a trial area had it remained independent.

Although Midland Red had been the largest operator in both counties – and indeed covering a huge area of the Midlands – for over half a century, Herefordshire (unlike Worcestershire) had an equally long tradition of independent operators running services in much of the area. Indeed Midland Red, even in its grandest days, had never penetrated sizeable parts of the county while there were several very old-established independent bus operators. It is worth mentioning that

Another early challenger to the accepted system was C K Coaches (Cardiff) Ltd which began running second-hand double-deckers on routes which competed with Cardiff City Transport services. Among the vehicles operated was this ex-London Transport Daimler Fleetline with MCW body, THM 552M, which entered service with LT as DMS552 in 1973 and was withdrawn by that organisation six years later. It is seen in April 1981 after being repainted in a white and orange livery reminiscent of that used by Greater Manchester PTE.

several had kept going some routes that did not pay long before the days of subsidies, as part of their sense of community in the areas they served. Most notably, there was Yeomans of Hereford, a family business founded in 1920 and running nineteen stage carriage routes by 1931, though it had gone through many changes over the years, running 26 buses and coaches and a minibus in 1981. Another family business with an equally long history was that of Bengry, trading as Primrose Motor Services, of Leominster, with twelve coaches and two minibuses. Morris of Bromyard was not so old-established, but had taken over a previous business with routes serving that locality.

Midland Red had been forced by circumstance to cut back on its more rural services several times – first in 1970-71 to cope with a financial crisis caused by rising costs and falling revenue suffered by much of the industry, then after the transfer of many of its most profitable routes (those operating within the West Midlands county then about to come into effect) to West Midlands PTE in 1973, and again as a result of a market analysis project (MAP) survey in mid-1980. The company was under heavy pressure to cut costs and was threatened with a reduced county subsidy. As usual, the aim was to rationalise services to improve loadings on those that remained. Inevitably the abandoned services, and also the fact that intending passengers were sometimes left behind

on the new network, gave rise to complaints to the county council and it has been suggested that this was also a factor in the decision to put forward the trial area proposal.

However, more immediately, the county, together with several independent operators, set about setting up replacement services and by the spring of 1981 there were eleven independent operators running from Hereford bus station, Yeomans having taken over stands previously occupied by Midland Red, while others included Morris of Bromyard, which had not previously operated into Hereford. Having co-operated in this way, there was shock on the part of operators when the idea of a trial area, with its implication that any operator could run on any route without regard for whatever service already existed. Quite a stormy meeting at Hereford Shire Hall ensued, but the scheme went ahead, the area designated covering most of Herefordshire except for an area towards the Gloucestershire and Welsh borders. It came into effect on 29th July 1981, with a two-year term, though the county council's contract tender system for subsidised services meant that changes were more related to the contract date of 1st October.

As it happened, the Midland Red Omnibus Co Ltd was split into four bus operating sections, plus coaching and engineering companies, with effect from 6th September 1981. Part of the aim – also reflected in other NBC reorganisations around that time – was

to relate the operating company areas more closely to county boundaries, a clear indication of the importance the county councils had acquired as the bodies responsible both in terms of financial support and in an organisational sense for ensuring that public transport was adequate. One of the four new companies was Midland Red (West) Ltd, responsible for the Hereford and Worcester area – the other new bus operating companies were identified similarly by the other points of the compass.

Many of the staff regretted the division for, despite its size and some difficult problems, Midland Red was one of those fortunate companies with a strong sense of staff loyalty. Its Hereford garage seemed to have no future, for the company decided not to participate in the tendering exercise on the grounds that the operator was less free than under the road service licensing system and that long-term planning was incompatible with relatively short-term contracts. Closure was in mind and accepted by the trade union, but local staff met and accepted cuts in pay quoted as over £40 per week, to keep the garage alive. This was done by working on a four-day week basis, extra payments for Saturday and Sunday working sacrificed and overtime paid on a flat-rate basis.

Midland Red (West) thus reduced its services from 21st September to a simplified network in Hereford and its immediate area, plus the trunk routes to Birmingham via Leominster and

Ludlow and Worcester via Bromyard. Evening and Sunday services were largely withdrawn. Considerable switching of services, not only from Midland Red to independents but between the latter, resulted from the tenders.

Among them were some relative newcomers, notably D. J. Whitehead, trading as Flashes Coaches, based about 20 miles away at Newent, in Gloucestershire. This concern had taken over a rural service in the county earlier in the year, and took over some Midland Red city services. It should be explained, perhaps, that Hereford has city status by virtue of its cathedral but has a fairly modest population of about 48,000. However, in December, Whitehead began competing directly with Midland Red (West) on Hereford local routes, mainly using a pair of ex-Leicester Bristol RE single-deckers together with a couple of other quite elderly vehicles. There were no local servicing facilities and the vehicles were left in the bus station overnight where they suffered some vandalism. Concern about roadworthiness led to a cut in the number of vehicles he was allowed to operate and the fact that his base was in the Western Traffic Area and the refusal of one in the West Midlands (which included Hereford) added to the difficulties. Ultimately, in February 1983 his licence was revoked. Yeomans took over some routes but other new independent operators appeared on others.

Competition between the various independents increased, and Primrose of Leominster began taking an active part in Hereford local services, leading to direct rivalry between Yeomans and Primrose, and old tricks common in the 'twenties but outlawed for half a century by the Road Traffic Act 1930 reappeared, such as 'nursing' a competitor's vehicle with one that runs just in front and also running a free bus five minutes ahead of the latter's timing.

A new operator appeared on the scene, W. D. Davies, trading as Stretton Coaches, starting in March 1983. Yeomans, to considerable surprise, gave up the 4.5 mile Credenhill-Hereford route – considered to be the only service in the county that was reckoned to be profitable – selling it to Midland Red (West). Ironically, it had been taken over from Midland Red as long ago as 1934. Stretton vehicles appeared on this route and others run by Midland Red (West). The latter retaliated by running an hourly yellow-painted bus with bold lettering 'Free Bus' – there were three buses on such departures, one requiring fares from both MR(W) and Stretton and the free bus – inevitably, passengers favoured the free bus as long as it continued.

There were numerous fluctuations of service, the frequency of Credenhill increasing from two to five buses per hour on weekdays and fares fluctuated wildly. It was obvious that this type of extreme competition could not continue for long and even if an operator who decided to withdraw or sell up was replaced by a fresh contender, the instability was confusing to passengers and was unlikely to lead to a long-term build-up of traffic.

In subsequent developments, much was made of an apparent saving in subsidies of £59,000 during the first year of the trial area. Much of this was because Midland Red would not participate in the contract scheme, but C. S. Dunbar suggests that the method of calculation is suspect. The network payment to Midland Red covering the whole county is thought to have been divided by the total mileage and the resulting figure multiplied by the Midland Red mileage in the trial area. Dunbar poses the question – if this is a correct way of working out the saving, why had such a large sum been paid to Midland Red in respect of services it could run without? A similarly large saving in the transport of schoolchildren was claimed but Dunbar points out that in the past, the county education department hired coaches in for this work regardless of existing stage services, whereas more use was now being made of the latter.

It was perhaps a case of the results of the experiment being presented in a way that appeared to prove the point that was sought, rather than a genuine unbiased study. Certainly, professional bus people found it hard to believe that the idea of one operator being free to attack the services of another in such a direct way was at all likely to create or even maintain an effective public transport network. It was foreseen that direct competition was likely to drive operators to seek minimum costs but, unless there was close scrutiny of their activities, standards were liable to drop

A succession of independent operators ran vehicles on the Hereford-Credenhill route, and when Stretton coaches, W. D. Davies, began operating on the route in direct competition to Midland Red (West) the latter retaliated by running a so-called 'free bus' on the same timings. The objective may have been to demonstrate the folly of complete deregulation, but Midland Red's 'aggressive attitude' was commented upon adversely in remarks made by independent operators and may have influenced subsequent Government policy. Seen here on the route in October 1983 is Stretton's VCJ 900J, a Bedford YRQ with Plaxton Panorama Elite 45-seat coach bodywork originally operated by Yeoman's and dating from 1971. The use of elderly vehicles, often purchased after completing a normal span of service from other operators, was to be typical of the type of operator encouraged by bus service deregulation.

During the early 'eighties there tended to be a conflict of view between the Government and the councils of the metropolitan counties that had been set up in 1974. The former was against the whole principle of public ownership and subsidy while the latter, in general, were strongly in favour. To a large extent this was a straightforward right-left divide, most of the councils being Labour, often of quite a left-wing kind, and the doctrinaire views taken up by each side tended to reinforce each other. This Greater Manchester MCW Metrobus photographed in May 1983 carries publicity for fares reductions of a kind then in favour in several PTE undertakings on the basis that subsidised fares would encourage use of public transport. The vehicle, No. 5038, was one of a batch of 50 Metrobus models of the Gardner-engined air-pressure brake type placed in service in 1981 – although GMT generally favoured Leyland chassis and Northern Counties bodywork, some 190 Metrobuses were also added to the fleet over the 1979-1983 period. Note the gradual departure from the original largely white and orange of SELNEC and early GMT days. The Metrobus is in an intermediate version and 7623, a P-registered Atlantean in the then current style.

and operators, especially inexperienced independent businesses, simply go out of business as they tried to cut expenditure to a point that is inadequate to maintain safety and reliability.

However, this wasn't how the trial area experiment was seen by the politicians who had set it up. This was very much in line with the thinking as publicly expressed even before the 1979 Election by Norman Fowler and hence he was simply following through the right-wing principles favoured by Mrs Thatcher. At that time, Government sources were particularly scornful of what was sometimes called 'the Soviet Republic of South Yorkshire' where the council of the metropolitan county set up under the reorganisation of local government in 1974 had adopted left-wing Labour philosophy and hence had built up a high-expenditure high-rates policy, much criticised by the management of local industry. However, the basic idea of providing public transport at low cost to the passenger as a means of combating both traffic problems and reducing pollution had wider appeal. South Yorkshire PTE operated under a specific policy of maintaining fares at a standardised level which had been achieved by 1976. In itself this was by no means unique – West Midlands PTE had adopted a similar policy under Conservative county administration in early 1973 (see page 49 of *Early 'Seventies – The Proof of the Pudding* in this series).

The cost of the scheme, including a subsidy to NBC operators in the area –

notably Yorkshire Traction – to allow them to set their fares at the same level, was not too great at first. However, the severe inflation of the time, which killed off West Midlands' similar venture, raised the cost to about £50 million per year by 1980, a very large sum by any standards. South Yorkshire's more hard-line political leaders took a quite determined line and the head-on clash with the Thatcher Government's philosophy of reliance on market forces to determine such matters as fares led to a mutual test of will-power.

Yet South Yorkshire could point to some benefit from its policies, even if difficult to measure in cost/benefit terms. By holding a typical journey from the outer suburbs to Sheffield city centre to 9p when comparable journeys in other cities were three or four times as much, passenger carryings were rising at about 4 per cent per annum by the end of the 'seventies. Reliability of service was claimed to be better because of reduced traffic congestion.

However, South Yorkshire may have damaged the case for financial support for public transport by its dogmatic nature – even its association with the very militant Yorkshire coal-mining community, the homeland of Arthur Scargill, helped to build up a picture of unacceptable extremism, as judged from Whitehall. Several other major cities or conurbations followed a policy of subsidising public transport to a lesser degree and there was a clear clash of policy between national and local government, especially as Labour tended to gain more strength after the

1981 local elections.

This was particularly manifest in London, where the clash of will between the Greater London Council based in its headquarters in County Hall diagonally across Westminster Bridge from the Houses of Parliament, described in the previous volume of this series, continued. Labour won the May 1981 Greater London Council election by a narrow margin, and a left-wing group proved to be dominant, installing Ken Livingstone as Leader, and David Wetzel, a former London bus inspector, as Chairman of the Transport Committee. The election had been fought on a manifesto which promised a 25 per cent cut in fares, labelling it the 'Fares Fair' programme.

This was put into effect and indeed exceeded in October 1981, when an average fare cut of 32 per cent was introduced. Soon there was an increase in the number of passengers using London Transport buses and trains daily from 5.5 million to 6 million and a small reduction in the numbers of cars on the streets, with useful benefit in traffic congestion. Inevitably, there was a cost, the subsidy from London's ratepayers going up by £125 million in a full year. Ratepayers – by no means all of whom used the transport system – complained, pointing out that many of those benefitting lived outside the GLC area and thus did not pay, though as usual with local expenditure, there was a substantial contribution from central Government to which general taxation contributed. Moreover the total level of subsidy, which had gone up from 29 per cent to 56 per cent of total costs, had become roughly similar to that in Paris (where it was not a matter of contention between the political parties to any significant extent).

It was in keeping with the times, and the emergence of a type of Conservatism equally militant to the Labour Left, that the Borough of Bromley, one of the leafier suburbs on London's south-eastern outskirts with a high proportion of car ownership, decided to challenge the 'Fares Fair' policy. It was taken through a series of court hearings and finally to the House of Lords, when it was ruled in December 1981 that the reduced fares were unlawful under the terms of the Transport (London) Act of 1969, which had set up the system of policy control of LT by the GLC. It was considered that LT had to plan to operate on a commercial basis, paying its way, so far as possible, in each year and if not achieving this, correcting any shortfall subsequently.

Inevitably, it was seen as a political decision, though the 1969 Act had been drafted at a time when the need for heavy subsidy if fares were to be kept

down was simply not foreseen – this was true also of the Transport Act 1968, and it is fair to point out that buses, in particular, had been expected to pay their way in most circumstances in Britain generally up to that time. Reluctantly, the GLC gave way and at the first possible date, 21st March 1982, an increase which virtually doubled London bus and tube fares (96 per cent increase) was introduced. The number of passengers carried fell, dropping to 5 million and street congestion worsened, but the cost to the ratepayers of London fell by £200 million in a full year.

It was widely agreed that the increase was excessive and the search for a more equitable method of dealing with the problem was taken up by David Howell, who had been appointed Secretary of State for Transport in succession to Norman Fowler in August 1981. With Government approval, the GLC re-examined the subject, including the commissioning of an opinion poll, and a direction for a 25 per cent cut was again issued by the GLC to LT in December 1982. London Transport itself challenged it this time, wary of

the damage done by the previous sequence of events. This time the High Court decided it was legal, largely on the grounds that it represented a reasonable compromise. Even so, there was a further period of doubt as the Transport Act 1983 authorised the Government's Transport Secretary to lay down guidelines for public transport subsidies by the GLC and also the metropolitan counties thus covering cases like that of South Yorkshire. If the guidelines were not met, the body responsible was liable to legal challenge and Government penalty.

The GLC sought advice again, but was advised it could go ahead, and the 25 per cent cut was put into effect on 22nd May 1983. This brought the average level of London fares back almost exactly to what it had been just before the 'Fares Fair' changes. Had there been a simple freeze, it might have passed unchallenged, but the experience had hardened the Government's attitude to the GLC control of London Transport. Indeed, the whole future of the GLC and the metropolitan counties was coming under question.

The London Transport 'Fares Fair' scheme was the subject of a major battle of wills between the Greater London Council and the Government. An average cut of 32 per cent in fares was introduced in October 1981, and was still in force when this snowy scene outside Euston station was photographed in January 1982. The Leyland-built Fleetline nearest the camera, DMS2346, and one of the Routemasters also visible carry posters advertising the scheme, the former listing 'Four new low bus fares' and the latter illustrating the GLC/LTE area in which it operated. The Fleetline had entered service in June 1978, when deliveries of this model to LT were almost ending. Withdrawals of earlier examples of the type were well under way, but the Routemasters marched on – RM721 on the left of the picture dated from April 1961 and thus had already over 20 years' service behind it.

After a couple of years when it had begun to seem that the drive for radical change of Mrs Thatcher's Government had gone off the boil, at least in regard to the bus industry, Nicholas Ridley's arrival on the scene as Secretary of State for Transport in October 1983 heralded the biggest changes in the British industry's structure and regulation, or the lack of it, since early horse-bus days.

Chapter five:
A new zealot

For a couple of years from the autumn of 1981 it seemed that the radicalism shown by Mrs Thatcher's Government was becoming somewhat tempered so far as the bus industry was concerned. The appointment of David Howell as Secretary of State for Transport in August 1981 brought a more subtle approach than that of Norman Fowler, as indicated by his method of dealing with the London 'Fares Fair' crisis described in the previous chapter.

It may well have been that the Greater London Council's activities diverted his attention from considering the bus industry's future as a whole as much as might have happened otherwise – his major legacy to it was the Transport Act 1983, which set guidelines for determining the financial policy for London Transport and the Passenger Transport Executives, which was to be agreed with the Government annually, with a three-year forward programme. It reflected the Government's growing desire to control local government purse-strings.

In April 1982, the Government's – and the country's – attention was diverted by the Argentine invasion of the Falkland Islands, and over the following months, the campaign to get them back. This tended to keep domestic policy out of the headlines, though there had been some discussion of 'privatising' NBC in the autumn of 1981. However, at that point what was in mind was the introduction of private capital into NBC, there being a reference to proposed legislation to permit this in the Queen's Speech setting out the Government's intentions in November 1981.

Even this was regarded with caution by Lord Shepherd, NBC's Chairman, who had been appointed in the final months of the Callaghan Government, taking office in January 1979. He had been the Labour peer given the responsibility of piloting the Transport Act of 1968 through the House of Lords, so was committed to the principles on which NBC was founded. Yet he was by no means dogmatic in his approach, and from the beginning had sought to make NBC as independent of Government interference as possible by encouraging it to stand on its own feet financially to the greatest extent. It even enabled him to work towards full privatisation, when that became a clear Government objective, though retaining the organisation's structure.

In those days, NBC had a very effective top-management team for, despite their different backgrounds, Lord Shepherd worked closely with Robert Brook, who had been appointed Chief Executive in January 1977. Robert Brook had begun his involvement with the bus industry in 1950, as an accountant with West Yorkshire Road Car Co Ltd, later becoming General Manager of the North Western and then Midland Red companies, before moving to NBC headquarters at New Street Square, in London. When Lord Shepherd's term of office ended in December 1984, Robert Brook succeeded him as Chairman, combining this post with that of Chief Executive until his resignation in April 1986.

London Transport tended to dominate the political scene so far as the bus industry was concerned in 1981-82, because of the Fairs Fare episode, but it had also been going through a period of difficulty on the vehicle side. Among these was the disruption in supply of the Leyland Titan integral-construction double-decker resulting from the decision to close the Park Royal works where the first 250 of the London vehicles had been built. Delivery had stopped in May 1980, the last vehicle, T250, having appeared at the Motor Show that year before entering service in November. Deliveries from Workington did not get under way again until March 1981, the first thirteen buses being built up using parts made by Park Royal, but nearly 300 entered service in 1982, including T563 dating from September, seen here in company with Routemaster RM247, in service since December 1962.

The General Election of June 1983 gave Mrs Thatcher her second term as Prime Minister, but David Howell was not included in the new Government. Almost his last action as Transport Secretary had been to announce proposals for the setting up of a new regional transport authority for London. His successor was Tom King, and if, as was suggested, David Howell had been dropped because of insufficient support for Thatcherite thinking, no dramatic change was evident from his successor,

who soon established himself as another politician willing to listen to professional expertise before taking action.

Even so, the twin principles of deregulation and privatisation continued to be in favour. Tom King was thinking along the lines of privatising NBC as a complete entity along similar lines as British Gas or British Telecom – Lord Shepherd recording in his contribution to the *NBC Commemorative Volume* how, in

private discussions, there had been agreement with Tom King and even Norman Fowler along these lines. This had not been made public, but in September 1983 Tom King gave a speech to the Bus & Coach Council (the new name adopted in 1982 for what previously had been best known as CPT, but whose full name was still the Confederation of British Road Passenger Transport) in which he referred to NBC as 'increasingly profitable' and stating that the idea of

By 1983, the National Bus Company had some reason to believe that it had adjusted to the new circumstances with considerable success and could look to the future with confidence, certainly if it was to be judged on commercial terms, returning its best profit figure that year, enough to remain the best of its career after heavy interest payments had been deducted. From the point of view of the public's impression, the National Express Rapide services were perhaps the most outstanding feature. This photograph emphasises that despite the up-market slant of better-equipped and more comfortable vehicles with hostess service, the main customers continued to be the young and the elderly, to both of whom low fares were essential. A Greenslades Leyland Tiger with Plaxton Paramount body is about to depart for London on a West of England service.

Relationships between local authority and nearby company undertakings varied considerably in character, from close co-operation to suspicion and antagonism. On Tyneside, there had been joint working of many services for over half a century and the opening of the Tyne & Wear PTE's Metro rapid transit rail system, on which a train is shown at Whitley Bay in March 1981, led to extensive replanning of local bus services, in which the two NBC subsidiaries, Northern General Transport Co Ltd, and United Automobile Services Ltd, were closely involved. Vehicles had begun to be painted in the PTE's yellow, but in NBC style, in the 'seventies but the full PTE's yellow and white livery was adopted for company buses running on routes within the area from 1981, as shown by the Northern company's Leyland Atlantean with Roe bodywork, 3484, and Leyland National 4555 seen here in Washington New Town in March 1984. Such co-ordination was out of favour under Nicholas Ridley's regime as Secretary of State for Transport.

introducing private capital required urgent attention – there was certainly no hint of breaking up NBC.

Less than a month later, however, fate intervened. The enforced resignation of Cecil Parkinson from the Government because of revelations concerning his relationship with his secretary caused a reshuffle of Cabinet posts. Tom King became Employment Secretary and Nicholas Ridley was appointed Secretary of State for Transport.

The Ridley family had been owners of coal mines in the north-east of England prior to their nationalisation by the Labour Government of 1945-50 and Nicholas Ridley was, and still is, a strong supporter of Mrs Thatcher and shares her philosophy of the merits of unregulated competition and the privatisation – one might almost say destruction – of State-owned businesses. His outlook was clear from the start and he set about putting his ideas into effect without delay. It was not long before the bus industry realised that it was dealing with someone determined to follow the Thatcher line and not receptive to any advice to the contrary.

The fact that the bulk of the management of the bus industry, probably overwhelmingly Conservative in their own personal political views even though managing publicly-owned organisations, were very unhappy about deregulation and, in many cases, the ending of the principle of cross-subsidy, had no effect. However, back-biting between different sectors, and criticisms of specific problems with the existing regime, was apt to be noted and used in support of the proposed changes.

It was unfortunate in this context, perhaps, that the old quarrels that tended to break out from time to time between some company undertakings, particularly certain NBC subsidiaries, and municipalities as well as independents were being highlighted in the months before the Ridley regime began. The House of Commons Select Committee on Transport had been

Beginning in 1976, a series of agreements involving Lancashire County Council, the NBC subsidiary in its area, Ribble Motor Services Ltd and local authorities which ran their own bus services in the county were signed, the aim being a uniform standard of services throughout the county. The level of service and fares were determined by the local authorities which received all the revenue from the fares, paying Ribble an agreed sum for operating those services it provided. The first agreement was with Burnley & Pendle Joint Transport Committee, and in this scene at Burnley bus station in April 1984, Leyland Nationals of both Burnley & Pendle and Ribble are seen on local services. The Burnley & Pendle vehicle was one of a batch of ten acquired from Tyne & Wear PTE in 1979—second-hand purchase of buses by major operators, once quite rare, were becoming much more common. Again, such joint agreements did not comply with the new thinking that unregulated competition was the solution to the transport industry's problems.

taking evidence on subsidies in March 1983 when D. G. F. Rawlinson, then NBC's Regional Director for the Northern Region, commented that, in his view, the municipal operator was 'substantially an anachronism' and claiming that it had to have support from rates because 'there is no way you can run an organisation of that size (he had referred to fleet sizes of fewer than 100 vehicles) in public transport and generate enough money to pay your bills'. One wonders, incidentally, what the typical independent operator thought of that remark.

The theme was taken up in an official NBC document that summer, suggesting that the local authorities' function was in planning rather than running public transport. It proposed an 'arm's length' relationship between those local authorities that owned bus undertakings and their day-to-day management, a concept that was to be picked up and formalised in the Government's subsequent legislation. Inevitably the Association of District Councils hit back, pointing out that local authorities were accountable to district auditors and that it was their efficient operation that allowed fares often to be lower than those of NBC companies. The fact that there were numerous instances of co-operation between operators of different types, quite apart from many effective joint agreements, was all too easily forgotten.

In regard to independent operators, when the House of Commons Transport Committee took evidence from the

participants in the Herefordshire Trial Area, the reports of aggressive behaviour of Midland Red (West) influenced the subsequent debate about the maximum size of concern which should be permitted to be sold off when NBC was to be privatised, according to Mr Peter Fry, MP.

More significantly, when Lord Shepherd and Robert Brook met Nicholas Ridley for the first time, they were shocked to discover how intransigent the latter was. Knowing

that he was likely to demand an element of competition, Robert Brook had outlined a scheme for three groups of local bus companies to take over from NBC. Ridley's reaction was to dismiss the idea as 'cuckoo' – thus began an increasingly uncomfortable spell of two-and-a-half years for Robert Brook, with increasing pressure for him to accept policy decisions, with many of which he profoundly disagreed.

It was not that NBC had proved reluctant to adopt radical ideas; some

Some NBC senior management took an antagonistic attitude to municipal operators, in one case criticising fleets of fewer than 100 vehicles as uneconomic. The Rhymney Valley District Council, despite itself being an amalgamation of three undertakings (Caerphilly, Gelligaer and Bedwas & Machen) had a fleet of 68 vehicles in the early 'eighties, including this 10-metre Leyland Leopard PSU4E/2R with Willowbrook 43-seat bodywork, No. 75, seen soon after entering service at Ystrad Mynach in August 1978. The Leopard had been chosen for about two-thirds of the fleet requirements, in either 10- or 11-metre form. The display of the fleetname in Welsh on the offside of the vehicle had become common practice in South Wales.

The NBC decision to experiment with intensive use of minibuses on urban services in Exeter as an answer to the threat of competition made a complete break with accepted principles of bus operation in Britain. The initial choice of vehicle was the Ford Transit, and a programme for conversion to 16-seat buses of the basic 'parcel van' body shell was put in hand at the Carlyle works of Midland Red. The resulting vehicle, with side windows produced by simple rubber glazing of apertures cut into the body sides, looked even more basic than earlier generations of passenger conversions of similar models dating back to soon after the first-generation Transit appeared in the mid-'sixties. With soap-packet styles of livery and lettering the 'cheap and cheerful' overall effect hardly tied in with the upmarket image claimed in the original report made to the NBC board in August 1983. One of the original vehicles, Devon General No. 24, is seen in Exeter in March 1984 just after the beginning of operation of the experimental services.

of Robert Brook's own views were and are quite controversial. One of the most significant proposals, made in August 1983, came from three of NBC's management directors – John Hargreaves Derek Fytche and Brian Barratt. It was that NBC should begin an intensive urban minibus service as an experiment, but with the intention of the adoption of the idea on a large scale if successful. The idea was quite revolutionary in Britain at the time, for minibuses had been seen generally as vehicles for use in small numbers on rural or specialised urban services, say where larger vehicles were unsuitable. Even so, it was accepted.

It was triggered by the application that had been made late in 1982 by Associated Minibus Operators Ltd (becoming better known as AMOS), a company headed by a former Hong Kong Traffic Commissioner, Anthony

Shephard, to run 500 minibuses, (leased on an individual basis to small concerns) on four routes running from the suburbs into London. It had been turned down, but the NBC team considered that a revised application might succeed and that other similar ventures might be set up by independent operators elsewhere. A smaller scheme, using five vehicles, had been approved by the Traffic Commissioners for operation in Luton.

It was considered that the minibus had 'an up-market universal appeal' while the 'lumbering stage-carriage' had a 'down-market image'. The report, reproduced in full in the *NBC Commemorative Volume*, conveys a note of alarm at the need to fight off the incursion of private operators on existing services, with a comment that costs had to be cut by at least a third on the basis of the competition experienced from full-sized buses in the Hereford

Trial Area.

It was proposed that 50 minibuses should be placed in service by Devon General Ltd in Exeter, and a fleet of Ford Transit 16-seat vehicles began to enter service in February 1984. The pros and cons of minibuses are examined in a later chapter, but there is no doubt that the NBC initiative, and its large-scale follow-up, was influenced by, as well as itself influencing, Government attitudes.

Before continuing with the course of events nationally, it is opportune to bring the story of events at London Transport up to date. Sir Peter Masefield's chairmanship of the London Transport Executive had been intended as a caretaker term of office when he was appointed in August 1980 but was extended twice before it ended in September 1982. It had been valuable in helping to rebuild self-confidence

The development of minibus services by NBC subsidiaries expanded greatly in subsequent years, nowhere with more enthusiasm than within Devon General Ltd itself. It became the first NBC bus-operating concern to be privatised in August 1986, under a management buy-out led by Harry Blundred, the company's Chairman and Managing Director, who spread the minibus gospel not only within the traditional operating territory–as here at Paignton in the Torbay area in May 1987 where vehicles carried the local fleetname Bayline – but also in competitive ventures in Oxford and London.

It was perhaps characteristic of the times that the world-famous title 'London Transport' was elbowed aside after half a century in 1984, for the London Transport Executive gave way to London Regional Transport, a curious name for a body which was to be little more than a holding company for the bus and Underground rail systems now to be operated as separate concerns. When this MCW Metrobus, M1008, entered service in April 1984, it was owned by LTE but LRT took over in June, just after this photograph was taken at the Euston terminus of the special Airbus service to Heathrow Airport, for which it was one of 24 vehicles specially adopted, with 43 coach seats on the upper deck and all but nine passenger seats on the lower deck removed to allow space for luggage. At the end of LTE's existence, it had roundly 1,000 apiece of the Leyland Titan and MCW Metrobus models, all under six years old. No remotely comparable renewal of London's bus fleet has occurred since, and the factories that built both, starved of orders from London and elsewhere, have closed.

within the organisation, for his style was one of involvement while allowing the expertise of his staff to come through. His successor was Dr Keith Bright, who had previously been in charge of the Huntley & Palmer biscuit and food business. His philosophy was one of cutting costs wherever possible without worsening the service to the public. Dr David Quarmby, who had been promoted from Director of Operational Research to become the youngest member of the LTE board of directors in the mid-'seventies, continued as Managing Director (Buses).

A noteworthy appointment at a slightly lower level within LT was that of Marcus Smith in February 1981, as General Manager (Buses). Previously he had been Engineering Director, having joined London Transport from Leyland in 1980 and being perhaps best known as what might be called 'father'

of the Leyland National.

However, the London story continued to be dogged by political activity. By 1983, the setting-up of a new structure to break the relationship with the Greater London Council was well under way, but the House of Commons Committee on Transport had put forward quite a far-reaching proposal in July 1982. It was that a Metropolitan Transport Authority should be set up, covering the old London Passenger Transport Area that had been recognised in the 1933-69 period, taking over London Transport and the metropolitan road system and setting up an organisation like that used in Hamburg, bringing in relevant British Rail and NBC activities. London Country Bus Services Ltd was thus being brought into the picture, partially reversing the hiving-off of its operations from London Transport which occurred

on 14th January 1970.

In practice, a much less ambitious idea emerged, and in the outcome only the name, London Regional Transport, gave a nod to the idea of responsibility for transport over a wider area which included that of many commuters. The Government's White Paper on this, issued in July 1983, simply spelled out the idea of LRT as a holding company for subsidiaries covering the ex-LT bus and Underground rail systems and directly responsible to the Secretary of State for Transport. Predictably, this prompted condemnation from the Greater London Council, to whom LT had reported since 1970.

Nicholas Ridley's arrival as Transport Secretary was just in time for him to deal with the AMOS appeal against the refusal of a licence to run 500 minibuses in London. He decided to allow it to go ahead, but the hearing

London Regional Transport was in control from 28th June 1984, Parliament having passed the Bill that brought it into existence. By September, M1441, one of the set of double-deckers of varying makes and specifications purchased in what was called an Alternative Vehicle Evaluation exercise, was newly in service and is seen near Lambeth Palace with the Houses of Parliament visible in the background. The vehicle was one of two Metrobus Mark II buses involved in the scheme and numbered to follow on from the total of 1,440 Metrobus Mark I models in service or still on order. Also visible is one of the Leyland National 2 single-deckers purchased in 1981 to replace the AEC Merlin buses previously used on the Red Arrow services linking main-line termini and shopping or business centres.

revealed such weaknesses in the proposals as to cause the Department of Transport inspector to condemn the scheme and, reluctantly, Nicholas Ridley had to concur.

The London Regional Transport Bill was published in December 1983 and enacted in June 1984. The GLC, under Ken Livingstone, was itself faced with extinction and had fought the loss of control by all means it could but London Regional Transport came into operation immediately on 28th June 1984. On 1st April 1985 the bus operating activities were transferred to a new subsidiary, London Buses Ltd, and vehicles henceforth carried this name as part of the legal lettering.

A major loss to the undertaking, and the bus industry generally, was Dr David Quarmby, whose resignation from the post of Managing Director (Buses) with LRT was announced in July 1984, taking effect in October, his new post being to take charge of distribution in the Sainsburys food store chain. He had been one of the first to see the possibilities of computers in transport concerns and had one of the liveliest minds in the business. It was clear he was unhappy with the trend of contemporary thinking.

The Ridley view of matters in general was already known when he took office but, in regard to the bus industry as a whole, a detailed picture of his intentions did not appear at first. Hence any comments such as those by the junior ministers in the Department of Transport were examined for clues as to the line to be taken. Mrs Lynda Chalker was Minister of State for Transport, with responsibility for bus policy among other duties, and so her comments during a speech at the Bus & Coach Council's Coaching Symposium in March 1984 were of particular interest. Naturally, much concerned the deregulation of coach services, but she put forward some fresh ideas on bus service control, though even at the time

The idea of cross-subsidising uneconomic but socially valuable services from profitable routes by requiring operators who wished to operate the latter to pay for franchises and transferring the money obtained to operators willing to run the loss-making routes was floated by Mrs Lynda Chalker, Minister of State for Transport early in 1984 but was out of line with the philosophy of Mrs Thatcher and Nicholas Ridley. In this scene in the Northumberland market town, Hexham, in June 1984, ETY 535L, a Plaxton-bodied Bedford YRQ of Tyne Valley Coaches Ltd bound for Haydon Bridge is seen in company with United Automobile Services Ltd 815 (APT 815W), a Bristol VRT with Gardner 6LXB engine and standard ECW 74-seat lowbridge body painted in Tyne & Wear PTE livery, standing in the bus station bound for Newcastle, about 20 miles away.

this seemed out of line with true Thatcherite thinking. The most striking of these was that services might be allocated on a franchise basis, operators having to pay for a franchise to run a profitable service, the money obtained thereby being used to subsidise loss-making services. Thus the idea of cross-subsidy would be retained, but the allocation would not have been in the hands of the operators, thus avoiding the accusation sometimes made that big operators tended to have an unfair advantage in the internal transfer of funds which could support an activity where a smaller competitor had no such advantage.

If I might introduce a personal note, I still regret that nothing more was heard of this idea, or something along similar lines. However, six months later the allocation of duties within the Department were altered and Mrs Chalker was no longer engaged on bus policy matters. Clearly her approach was not in favour, though she was later to find good use for her organisational talent when a later reshuffle caused her to become Minister of Overseas Development.

The White Paper outlining Nicholas Ridley's proposals, given the disarmingly simple title 'Buses', was published in July 1984. It was clear that deregulation, privatisation and competition were to be the watchwords. The main proposals were:-

* Road service licensing to be abolished throughout Great Britain except, for the time being, in London.

* NBC to be reorganised into free-standing parts, which were then to be sold off.

* The PTEs to be required to break down their operations into smaller units, which would become independent companies. Municipal bus operations to become companies owned by their district council. After a transitional period, PTE and municipal companies to stand on their own feet, competing with other operators.

* Local authorities to seek competitive tenders for contracts to run bus services not provided by the free market.

* Quality and safety standards to be maintained and tightened. Concessionary fare schemes to continue – all operators were to be entitled to participate in them. Additional resources to foster public transport in rural areas. Taxis and hire cars to be allowed to carry passengers at separate fares in certain circumstances.

For the time being, the Scottish Bus Group was not to be included in the privatisation process.

The reaction to all this from leaders of the bus industry, both operating and manufacturing, was almost universally hostile. I have a vivid recollection of attending the Bus & Coach Council Conference held in Blackpool in September 1984 and listening first to Nicholas Ridley, who claimed that his proposals had the passengers' interests in mind but also revealing a major motivation in his comment that revenue support for bus services, 'almost

unheard of' fifteen years earlier, amounted to over £500 million in the previous year. (It was already clear, incidentally, that drastic reduction of this, like other subsidies, was a prime aim on the Government's part). Yet fares had kept well ahead of inflation. A free competitive market was to be the means of getting a bus network based on people's needs. Cross-subsidy was 'the greatest vice of the present system' – it was hardly a coincidence that Mrs Chalker had just been moved to other duties.

In the discussion which followed, representatives of London Transport, the PTEs, municipal operators (including a local Conservative Councillor of 50 years standing with clear recollections of how the Road Traffic Act of 1930 had begun a 10-year process of 'building order out of chaos'), independents and manufacturers all spoke against the proposals. NBC representatives doubtless felt inhibited, and though no doubt some of the independents were broadly in favour, no-one spoke in favour of the blanket deregulation proposed. My overwhelming impression of that meeting was of Mr Ridley's air of disdain – it was clear that nothing would convince him that these people, most of whom had devoted a lifetime to the industry, might have some valuable advice.

It was at about that time, though not at the BCC Conference, that Mr Ridley began to make comments comparing bus operation with running a corner

The main target for destruction in Nicholas Ridley's proposals as outlined by his White Paper Buses of July 1984 was the National Bus Company, which was not merely to be privatised but split into individual operating companies to be sold off separately. Contrary to the trend in the 'seventies, it was considered that smaller units were preferable and some splitting of existing organisations was already well in hand. The Provincial Bus Co Ltd of Fareham, Hants, came into operation on 1st April 1983, taking over the activities of the former Gosport & Fareham Omnibus Co (which had used the fleetname 'Provincial', derived from its origins as part of the Provincial Tramways group) and the local operations of Hants & Dorset Motor Services Ltd, the main part of which became Hampshire Bus Co Ltd. The Gosport & Fareham company would probably have been absorbed into Hants & Dorset when acquired by NBC in 1969 but for the fact that it was a statutory company and so the name survived into the privatisation era. The Leyland National shown, seen in Southampton in September 1985, was one of seven from the same batch acquired from London Country in 1984.

shop. Yet it seems remarkable that someone with formidable powers of debating could not see the fundamental differences. Not even a greengrocer or fishmonger has to deal with such a perishable commodity as selling passenger miles – if the passenger doesn't board the bus before it leaves the stop, the wastage is immediate and complete. Moreover, even a none-too-competent shopkeeper of the style portrayed by the television comedy 'Open All Hours' can rely on the support of people in the immediate neighbourhood to some degree, simply because his premises are near at hand. Direct competition between bus operators is quite different – almost as

if a competitor's mobile shop had been parked immediately outside Mr Arkwright's shop – and passengers tend to board the first bus that comes along going in their direction, barring some unusually strong incentive to do otherwise, so the damage to the viability of one service by the appearance of a second is immediate.

In practice, if two or more operators on a route compete directly, it is usually not long before there are clear winners and losers. The latter will not be able to continue thus for long and the situation is inherently unstable. However, in the ensuing months, no-one was able to deflect the course to which Mr Ridley was committed, save in detail or timing

and most of what was envisaged in the *Buses* White Paper duly came to pass.

A Transport Bill embodying the proposals was laid before Parliament on 31st January 1985 and enacted as the Transport Act 1985 on 30th October 1985. Its provisions came into force at various dates in 1986 though the process of acting upon them continued during the following years. In the course of translating the ideas outlined in the White Paper into specific law, a number of new features became evident. Some were quite minor in themselves, though unfamiliar and causing changes to the day-to-day terminology used by bus operators and others interested in their activities.

The archaic-sounding but long-familiar phrase 'stage-carriage service' was replaced by the simpler 'local service', defined as one on which passengers can board and alight throughout its length for journeys of less than fifteen miles – they can be of any length in total. There were still to be Traffic Commissioners, but only one for each Traffic Area instead of three (previously the correct term for the permanent official was the Chairman of Traffic Commissioners, who sat in company with two lay Commissioners). The holder of a public service vehicle operator's licence could, from 26th October 1986, operate a local bus service anywhere, except in the London area, simply by registering it with the Traffic Commissioners. No system of allowing for objection to the service continued, though if police or a local authority responsible for traffic flow considered it necessary, conditions relating to safety or traffic could be applied. In general, a 42-day period of notice applied, both to start a new service or to end or alter an existing one, though there were special transitional arrangements during 1986 during the period of changeover from new to old systems.

This seemed a simple procedure, yet when the paperwork began to be issued, the steps to be taken become more complex. Some of this was straightforward notification, but an aspect of the new era which gradually loomed larger was the removal of the exemption to the Trade Practices Act 1976, relating to what was liable to be seen as anti-competitive action, which formed a part of the Transport Act 1985, the full implications of which were not widely realised at first. The basic idea of avoiding unfair ways of trading sounded innocent enough, but it began to be realised that the numerous joint services in which most medium-sized or large concerns were involved, often with several partners in surrounding areas, had to be registered, as did any agreements concerning fares or any on 'the extent to which services are made available' (this latter implying the ending of the area agreements which had been a key feature of the British bus industry, often with over half a century behind them).

Not only was this a further complication but it was made clear that any such agreement might be referred to the Restriction Practices Court. In a curious kind of way, the new 'freedom' had acquired more than a little of the kind of menace conveyed by George Orwell's novels, in which Big Brother was liable to intervene in practices which operators, in their innocence, had thought were primarily helpful to the public. But of course the idea that buses should be regarded primarily as a public service rather than simply a means of making money did not fit the Government's dogma.

An aspect of the Transport Act 1985 which received little publicity before it came into force was the full effect of the removal of the exemption from the Trades Practices Act 1976. It came as a considerable shock to many people in the industry that joint operation of services, previously generally regarded as logical and preferable from the public's viewpoint in providing and evenly-spaced timetable, was now regarded with suspicion. There were numerous instances of joint working in the North Western Traffic Area, partly because of the large number of local authority fleets but also because of long-standing friendly relations between different types of operator. A good example of this was the joint working of several routes south of Preston by J. Fishwick & Sons Ltd of Leyland, an independent operator, and Ribble Motor Services Ltd, an NBC company. Seen leaving Preston bus station for Earnshaw Bridge via Leyland on one of these in 1980 is Leyland Titan demonstrator FHG 592S, which was being operated by Fishwick for an extended period at the time. Several Ribble vehicles are visible on the left.

The year 1980 was the last in a run of five years when annual deliveries of buses and coaches to British operators had exceeded 5,000 and was a peak year for double-deck deliveries in recent history, with a total of 2,276 placed in service, though 1981 was almost as impressive in this sector at 2,210. Market leader by a hair-breadth was the Bristol VRT, with 604 delivered, this model just beating the MCW Metrobus at 602, though the Leyland Atlantean was not far behind at 579. The position of the VRT was almost entirely due to NBC orders, boosted by that organisation's revived emphasis on double-deckers as a consequence of its MAP route replanning programme. Seen here at Bournemouth in August 1985 is Wilts & Dorset 3448 (KRU 848W), one of a batch with Gardner 6LXB engines and ECW bodywork of the 74-seat low-height pattern used in most NBC fleets originally supplied to Hants & Dorset but most of which passed to Wilts & Dorset when the latter once again became a separate company on 1st April 1983.

Chapter six:
An autumn glow for manufacturers

The manufacturing side of the industry was having a better year than might have been expected in 1980, despite general economic gloom, and looking back from about twelve years later the figures of vehicles placed in service seem like a far-off dream by comparison with those of today. The strongest group was that of double-deckers, with some 2,276 delivered that year, according to Paul Heel's analysis for The Omnibus Magazine, the source of many interesting figures. There were two main reasons for what was even then a remarkable figure, higher than any in previous years since the mid-'sixties.

One was the signalled tapering-off of the new bus grant, and indeed 1980 was the last year in which it was to be at the full 50 per cent that had applied since 1971, so clearly it paid to get new buses on the road even a little ahead of actual need. Demand was also heightened by the National Bus Company's MAP route reorganisation schemes, which had put the emphasis back on to double-deckers as the most economic vehicles on route networks that were designed to be self-supporting. In addition, there was in many cases a backlog of vehicles on order from the previous year's programme, itself a sign of demand, though also partly due to production problems, notably with Leyland's rear-engined Titan and, inter-related with that, the closure in July 1980 of Park Royal Vehicles Ltd, which only a few years previously had been the largest producer of double-deck

Single-deck bus demand, previously running at over 1,000 vehicles per year nationally, began to drop in 1980, when 873 were delivered to British operators. This caused concern, but was trivial by comparison with what was to follow – by 1984 it had fallen to an incredible-seeming 131. The Leyland National 2 went into production in 1980, readily distinguishable by its more rounded windscreen and grille for the front-mounted radiator. The Yorkshire Traction Co Ltd was one of few NBC operators to build up a substantial fleet – No. 211 (EDT 211V) was one of 26 supplied in 1980, built to 11.6-metre length 52-seat form with the more utilitarian Standard Duty specification, lacking the roof pod heating and ventilating unit in a manner reminiscent of the series B version of 1978-80. It is seen at Rotherham in August 1981.

bodywork in the UK.

The single-deck bus picture was not so rosy, and indeed was giving concern, though the figure of 873 full-sized vehicles was to be the best achieved in the 'eighties. The comparable figures for previous years had not dropped below 1,000 since the late 'sixties, and the fall was again largely related to the MAP revisions, against which the bus grant effect did not have comparable influence.

The coach side of the industry was not generally influenced by new bus grant (save for those cases where vehicles built to a suitable specification were used on stage carriage duties for at least half their mileage). The recession that was beginning to bite could have been expected to show up in reduced demand for new vehicles, and indeed it did, but the drop was as yet modest compared to the previous year. The figure of 2,268 may have held up rather better than could have been expected, probably because of a short-term effect of coach deregulation, which enabled various new express services to be started by both the nationalised NBC and SBG organisations and the independents.

Inevitably, development of new models is based on decisions taken some years earlier and the radically different political climate, itself not clear in its effects on the transport industry at first, took some time to have effect. Moreover, the structure of the manufacturing industry itself continued to reflect the thinking of the 'seventies.

The British Leyland Motor Corporation was still almost entirely State-owned, and there was also the link with NBC which put the Leyland National plant at Lilyhall near Workington, the factory of Bristol Commercial Vehicles at Brislington, Bristol, and the Eastern Coach Works bodybuilding plant at Lowestoft into the Bus Manufacturers (Holdings) Ltd sub-group, jointly owned by Leyland and NBC.

Quite apart from this direct interest held by NBC in manufacturing facilities, there was strong influence on design. Oddly enough, this was perhaps less so with the Leyland National (originally developed by Leyland as a 'city bus' before NBC came into the picture with the agreement that gave it its name in 1969 and led to the building

Total coach sales, at 2,268, were still quite buoyant in 980, even if not as strong as in 1979, when the figure of 2,629 had been reached. A striking feature was the climb in sales of Volvo's B58 model, of which fewer than 100 per year had been sold up to 1978. In 1979 the total climbed to 215 and then nearly doubled again to 399 in 1980, almost all going to independent operators. At that stage, this was still behind Bedford and Ford, but was catching up rapidly and had already overtaken the Leyland Leopard among sales to this type of operator. Florence Grange Tours Ltd, of Morecambe, was a member of the Battersby-Silver Grey group of companies rather typical of the often complex structure of the coach business in Lancashire. The vehicle shown, one of a pair of 11-metre B58 models with Duple 49-seat bodywork, dated from September 1979.

of the factory and the beginning of production in 1972) then the two important new models introduced in 1980-81, the Olympian and the Tiger.

In a way, the Leyland Olympian double-decker could be described as a second-guess exercise, even though it was to prove one of the most successful bus models of any type in the 'eighties and appears to have a firm future even today. Leyland had intended the B15 project, later christened Titan, to be its new-generation double-decker when consultation with likely major users had begun in the early 'seventies, but it was influenced strongly by London Transport, incorporating two features –

independent front suspension and power-hydraulic braking – to which LT was strongly committed but which were not widely favoured elsewhere. It was also of integral construction, and this limited its appeal for some markets, such as Scotland, where there was a strong pressure to give work to a bodybuilder within that country, quite apart from overseas business.

There had been numerous problems in getting the Titan into production and initial interest in it from several PTEs and NBC had withered away almost completely, leaving it as virtually a London Transport 'special'. Meanwhile, the 'first generation' rear-

engined double-deckers had soldiered on – the Leyland Atlantean, originally introduced in production PDR1/1 form in 1958, though much improved in detail in the AN68 version from 1972; the Fleetline, originally introduced by Daimler in 1960, comfortably the market leader in the early 'seventies (over 1,100 had entered service in 1973) though demand for the later examples, built at Leyland from 1974, had dropped considerably before chassis production ended in 1980, and the Bristol VRT, put into production in 1968 but of similar general concept and owing an upsurge in demand largely to increased NBC emphasis on double-deckers.

The Olympian, at first known by the code B45, had been developed as a successor to all three, whose production was in any case due to end because impending legislation changes would have required uneconomic changes in design. However, it is fair to say that NBC had a particular influence with its requirement for a low-floor capability to permit a low overall height, particularly important in quite a number of its subsidiaries where bridge height made it impossible to use the 'normal' 14ft. 6in. height on some routes – a 'universal' model of about 13ft. 8in. was considered essential. So a rigid front axle and air-pressure brakes were adopted, while the use of a separate chassis, to be built at Bristol, meant that ECW could build the body, as also favoured by NBC. This also suited both SBG and Strathclyde PTE, which could have their buses bodied by Alexander, again as usual.

A further widening of the model's potential market followed from the design of the frame in a modular form with a variable-length centre-section. Initially 9.5 and 10 metre versions were offered, but clearly there was scope for further development. Some nine prototypes were built, all but one of which were delivered to operators (half of them overseas) during 1980-81. This in itself was a widely-welcomed change of method, contrasting with the lack of operator involvement in the Leyland National.

Normal production began at Bristol early in 1981 and by about the middle of the year completed vehicles were beginning to arrive with operators. It was almost immediately obvious that it was going to be more successful than the Titan, not merely in numbers but in breadth of the market covered. Yet, in fairness, it inherited a good deal of its mechanical design from that model, including much of the drive train, with the choice of Gardner 6LXB or Leyland

The choice of Olympian for what at first had been known as Leyland project B45 seemed odd, reviving memories of association with MCW, makers of the rival Metrobus. The previous Olympian had been a joint Leyland-MCW model, effectively an integral-construction version of the Tiger Cub light single-decker of the 'fifties, of which only limited numbers had been built. The heavier-duty Leyland-MCW Olympic single-decker was much better known, and had remained in quite large-scale production, mainly for export until the late 'sixties, being effectively swept aside by the Leyland National, which ended a long period of co-operation between Leyland and MCW. However, the name proved an appropriate choice when a 10-metre left-hand demonstrator was built for Athens, original home of the Olympic Games, in 1981. It was the 52nd production Olympian, and had a Leyland TL11 engine and bodywork by ECW. An order for nineteen similar buses was delivered in 1983.

TL11 engine (the latter a modernised equivalent to the 680 used in the Atlantean), and Self-Changing Gears Hydracyclic gearbox. The rear axle differed, however, being a drop-centre unit to permit low-height bodywork. The standard ECW or Roe body designs also showed Titan influence, yet particularly in the low-height form widely favoured by NBC seemed better proportioned.

Initially, deliveries of the earlier models continued. Indeed the Atlantean had an astonishingly good year in 1981, the delivery of 670 improving not only on 1980 but on any year in the 'seventies. Output diminished thereafter, but 284 were delivered in 1982, 145 in 1983

The ability to fit Scottish-built bodywork had been a reason for preference for separate body and chassis north of the border, but in the event Lothian Regional Council and Strathclyde PTE broke their long-standing allegiance to Alexander bodywork for batches of Leyland Olympian buses delivered early in 1982-83. Seen here is Strathclyde LO24, one of 25 vehicles with ECW bodywork supplied in 1983 – there had been strong competition to secure work for ECW, under growing financial pressure, but the subject was very controversial in Scotland.

The MCW Metrobus was the rising star among double-deckers at the beginning of the 'eighties, shooting up far beyond the modest success in the mid-'seventies of its predecessor, the Metropolitan, with deliveries above 600 per year in 1980 and 1981, beating all other models in the latter year, and attracting orders from a wide variety of operators. Newport Borough Transport had been a regular customer for the generation of MCW buses based on Scania mechanical units, both the Metro-Scania single-decker and the Metropolitan, but turned to the Gardner-engined Metrobus for sixteen vehicles, although then reverting to Scania chassis with other bodywork. Number 80 (JBO 80W) is seen in Cardiff in April 1981 soon after entering service.

and 134 in 1984, the final year for the model – production had to end because of noise emission and braking legislation. The passing of the model was regretted by many operators. The Bristol VR was sharply down in 1981 (it had just managed to be top model in 1980, with 604 deliveries), at 390 but it had been directly superseded on the production line by the Olympian, of which 89 had been bodied and delivered by the end of the year. Although the last Fleetline chassis were built in August 1980, bodybuilders were still delivering examples, amounting to 34 in 1981 and indeed four more entered service in

1982 and again in 1983. The Titan was by then in production at Workington, after the transfer from Park Royal, 132 being delivered. Thus, British Leyland's overall double-deck bus deliveries in 1981 were 1,315, just under 60 per cent of the total deliveries to United Kingdom operators that year, just 3 per cent down on the previous year's peak. In its first full year, 1982, Olympian deliveries were 370 and in 1983 a peak of 477 made it market leader – by that date total demand was falling.

Easily the largest challenger in the double-deck field, and indeed, in terms of individual models, the market leader

in 1981 and 1982, was the MCW Metrobus which just beat the Atlantean into first place with 677 deliveries in 1981; the 1982 figure was well down at 376 but still enough to beat the Olympian's rising output that year. This venture, MCW's first at building a complete vehicle without the help of a 'chassis' maker, had been quite remarkably successful since its introduction in 1977. In many ways it was a rival to the Titan, and indeed secured orders for London Transport directly comparable to those for the Titan, quite an achievement for a new model, though it did well elsewhere,

A number of major operators ran programmes in which new types of vehicle were the subject of comparative tests, so as to obtain experience on which future orders could be placed. Seen at an open day at Greater Manchester Transport's Hyde Road works in March 1983 are 1448, one of three Volvo Ailsa B55 models, 1461, a Scania N112DH, and 3006, one of an initial batch of ten Leyland Olympian models, all with Northern Counties bodywork, in company with the former 1080, one of the Mancunian design of double-deckers, in this case a Leyland Atlantean with Park Royal body, placed in service by Manchester City Transport in 1969 and pensioned off for other duties after service with both SELNEC and GMT. Also visible is the preserved Leyland Lion PLSC of Ribble Motor Services, visiting for the event. During this period GMT also ran Dennis Dominator and Falcon, and Volvo Citybus double-deckers on an experimental basis.

The Dennis Dominator was another beneficiary of the increase in demand for double-deckers, even if not in as great numbers as the Leyland or MCW models. The Scottish Bus Group had continued a more open attitude to competing makes than NBC from earlier periods and in the early 'eighties was taking batches of several makes. The Central SMT Co Ltd was the Group's largest Dominator user, following up a single vehicle with 20 more in 1981, putting them into use on new routes running across Glasgow in June of that year. They had Alexander bodywork of the newly-introduced R-type. Seen in Argyle Street is D9. Further batches brought the Central company's total of Dominators to 51 by 1983.

too. Its concept was slightly more orthodox, with what amounted to a separate chassis and a beam front axle but air suspension was standard and operators could choose air-pressure or power-hydraulic brakes, the latter by Clayton Dewandre, of a different type using higher pressure than the Lockheed system of the Routemaster and Titan. The Gardner engine, usually the 6LXB, was standard, as was Voith automatic transmission.

Next in line was the Dennis Dominator, another model introduced at about the same time as the Metrobus and usually with the Gardner-Voith combination, but, as introduced, slightly more basic with leaf-spring suspension (though air suspension became more usual later) and seen by many as a successor to the Fleetline, an image perhaps helped by the presence of Bob Crouch in charge of sales, just as he had been with Daimler in the Fleetline's most successful days. The Dominator was aimed more especially at municipal fleets, though there were sales to almost

all types of operator, and numbers had built up steadily, reaching 128 in 1981, and 192 in 1982; South Yorkshire PTE was the largest customer, though in that case the Rolls-Royce Eagle engine was favoured for the largest order of 174.

The odd-man-out in design terms was the Ailsa, which by that date was marketed as the Volvo B55. Its front-engined layout was the result of co-operation between the Scottish Bus Group and Ailsa Bus Ltd, Volvo's agent for the United Kingdom, resulting in the production of a batch of pre-production prototypes in 1974. Outwardly, it looked much like other modern double-deckers, the compact Volvo TD70 6.7-litre engine being mounted to the left of the driver yet allowing a front entrance platform in the usual way. The SBG ordered batches, though not in very large numbers and not to the exclusion of the Fleetline, also supplied to the Group's fleets in the late 'seventies in some quantity. Some PTE and municipal interest added to demand, especially in

later years, but by the early 'eighties, output was running at around 75 per year.

Mention should also be made of Scania, which returned to the British double-deck market at the 1980 Motor Show, but that venture belongs to a wider development covered in the next chapter.

Single-deck decline

Among single-deck buses, the Leyland National was still dominant in 1980, with 593 examples delivered in Great Britain, most being of the Leyland National 2 type with Leyland 680 engine then newly in production, accounting for two-thirds of total single-deck bus deliveries – a little under 300 of these were for NBC subsidiaries, only half the typical intake during the late 'seventies, yet it was to collapse almost completely over the following two years

– total sales of the model to all operators dropped below 100 in 1982 and never recovered. In its final years orders for London Transport, the PTEs and some municipalities took quite a sizeable share of output. The problem was not with the vehicle – it was generally agreed that the National 2 was a better machine than its smaller-engined predecessor, though rather noisy within – simply that the market for this type of vehicle was dropping almost to vanishing point.

The other contenders for single-deck bus business in 1980 were the Leyland Leopard (by then primarily a coach model, but still favoured as a bus by the Scottish Bus Group despite taking some National 2 models in 1980-81, and several municipalities). The light Bristol LH was ending production, though the short LHS was to continue on a small scale, and operators looking for lighter chassis for bus work, including some NBC fleets as well as independents, tended to favour the Bedford YMQ or YMT – the Ford was rather dropping out of favour for such work. The heavier-duty Seddon Pennine VII with Gardner engine had been favoured for both coach and bus work by SBG up to 1980 but then faded from the scene, whilst among independents the Volvo B58, though primarily a coach model was favoured by a few of the better-funded firms for bus work.

Dennis had been trying to build up its single-deck business and a handful of Dominators with single-deck bodies had been supplied to municipal fleets in 1979-80. The Falcon I chassis, introduced in September 1980, had a Gardner 6HLXB horizontal engine mounted at the rear and a Voith automatic gearbox mounted a short distance in front of the rear axle, the drive thus being taken forward and back again in a manner reminiscent of the Bristol RE. Indeed, it is not too much of an exaggeration to say that it was intended to fill the market vacuum created by British Leyland's insistence on dropping the well-regarded RE to concentrate business on the National. Just who though of the idea first is a matter for conjecture, but Geoffrey Hilditch, at the time General Manager of Leicester City Transport, could be described as being on friendly terms with the company, having encouraged its return to the bus business with the Dominator. However, Dennis's own management team was strong, with David Hargreaves as Chairman and John Hood on the engineering side, quite apart from Bob Crouch on sales, as already mentioned.

The Falcon with Gardner 6HLXB engine did appeal to several municipal fleets, but the numbers built were not large, simply because of the falling market. It was planned from the start to have variations, the Falcon II being powered by a Mercedes-Benz V6 engine and the Falcon III by a Perkins V8; it

The original concept of the Dennis Falcon could be described as a response to British Leyland's withdrawal of the Bristol RE model. The same design reasoning, of using a rather complex transmission layout to facilitate the use of the rather bulky Gardner engine under the floor at the rear, was employed and quite a number of operators showed interest, though actual sales numbers were modest because of the general drop in demand for single-deckers. Leicester City Transport was an 'obvious' user of what was at first called Falcon I but later became Falcon H (for horizontal engine) – though even this fleet only built up a fleet of seven, all with Duple Dominant bus bodies – No. 95, seen here, was one of the final three dating from 1984.

was also offered as a double-decker as well as a coach, more on which later in this volume.

However, Dennis also introduced a new lighter single-decker called the Lancet (to those with memories of earlier days, it was a little confusing since the Lancet and Falcon models of the 'thirties and 'forties were in an opposite relationship in terms of size and weight). This was more in the Bristol LH category, though in terms of layout, with vertical engine mounted amidships, it resembled Bedford passenger models – the engine on early versions was the Perkins T6.354, and an Allison automatic gearbox was

offered, though in typical Dennis fashion, a variety of options was available. Sales of this model were modest, too, though Merseyside PTE took ten in 1983. The days of Dennis resurgence as a maker of single-deckers were yet to come, but its ventures in a depressed market, plus the successes at home and abroad of its double-deckers, kept the firm alive as a challenger.

Coaches – a trend to heavies

Overall single-deck demand did not fall so dramatically because of

continued demand for coaches even though these too showed quite a sharp drop from a peak of 2,629 in 1979 to 1,542 in 1981 (significantly, this was the first full year of coach deregulation) though there was a recovery to 1,871 in 1983 before a further fall occurred. Chassis that could be used for either coach or bus work had an obvious overall sales advantage, and Leyland was able to claim first place among individual single-deck models for the Leopard in 1980, some 668 being sold that year.

This was quite a landmark, for Bedford, previously dominant as a supplier of coach chassis, had third

The Leyland Leopard had been steadily gaining in popularity and became the most popular single-deck model on the British market in 1980, quite an achievement for what was basically a 20-year old design, even though steadily developed. Part of its success was due to its suitability for either bus or coach duties, an aptitude bridged by vehicles such as this PSU3F/4R, one of ten with Willowbrook 003 Express 49-seat bodywork supplied to United Automobile Services Ltd in 1980. The NBC companies were beginning to back away from the tight conformity to the standardised corporate image livery styles by the time this photograph of No. 6235, bound for Carlisle in the Cumbrian village of Brampton, was taken in May 1984, and the original dual-purpose livery of red up to the waist and white above had given way to this style.

Over the years, coaches on 'light' and 'heavy-duty' chassis had become almost indistinguishable to the general public. While this might have been thought an advantage to the former, the first cost advantage also tended to diminish as specifications grew closer and operators found that more intensive use showed up the lower maintenance costs of good heavy-duty models. Some operators, such as Barton Transport, of Chilwell, Nottingham, then the largest surviving independent operator with substantial local as well as long-distance services, continued to buy both categories of vehicle. Here 524 (ARB 524T) a Bedford YMT of later 1979 is seen with 537 (ERB 537T) a Leyland Leopard PSU3E/4 of 1980 in Loughborough in November 1981. Both had Plaxton Supreme Express bodywork.

place (behind the Leyland National) with a little over 500 of the YMT model. Perhaps it would be fairer to consider total Bedford sales at 715 in 1980, for the YLQ and YMQ 10-metre model were virtually short-wheelbase equivalents to the YMT, but the total also included the venerable VAS 29-seat model first seen in 1962 and the even older SB, though that had virtually become an export-only model.

Even so, Bedford and Ford were losing ground to a serious degree. Bedford's fall for 1981 can only be described as catastrophic, its total dropping to 367 – in 1979 it had been 937, and in the 'seventies it had never fallen below 800. Ford had less far to fall, but its 1980 and 1981 figures of 522 and 306 were not encouraging.

Even worse was to follow – Bedford's totals for 1982 and 1983 were 285 and 183, while Ford dropped to 203 and 137.

The explanation for this lies in a combination of factors, but even so, the virtual collapse of demand for such vehicles was astonishingly rapid, especially when it is recalled how Bedford had dominated the independent coach business for almost half a century. Back in the early 'thirties, this had been based on being able to offer a small 20-seat model that gave good performance and, in terms of engine smoothness, better than average refinement with good reliability at low cost. Gradually the size increased and the price differential for complete vehicles became less marked as the bodywork

on the 'light' chassis became almost identical to that on 'heavy' models. By the late 'fifties Ford had emerged as a serious challenger, making models of similar concept, and sharing components with mass-produced goods models in a similar way. Bedford moved the engine to a mid-underfloor position for its larger models for 1970-72 which Ford left at the front, though below floor level from 1978.

Though both firms had broadly kept up with technical development – Ford was an early user of turbocharging, for example – they ran into a period in the 'sixties and 'seventies when reliability began to be judged inadequate. This was at least partly due to the intensive high-speed use made possible by the spread of motorways, when a heavier-

The Ford R-series, with its front-mounted engine, was becoming increasingly out of step with the times, even though a 1978 redesign, with the cylinders inclined to the left, meant that standard coach bodywork needed no protrusion above floor level. In essentials, this was a mid-'sixties design but Ford had been an early user of turbocharging to give an acceptable performance from the 6.0-litre engine, aided by a choice of six- or eight-speed Ford-manufacture all-synchromesh gearboxes. This R1114 example was used for publicity pictures at the time of the 1980 Show, having a Plaxton Supreme IV 53-seat body.

duty model like the Leyland Leopard or, increasingly, a Volvo B58, would prove a better proposition overall, even though more expensive to buy. However, both Bedford and Ford, part of combines mainly engaged in mass-produced car manufacture with headquarters in the United States, were apt to be unresponsive to the need for quite simple changes in design. There was also a sluggishness in response to the coach industry's growing interest in 12-metre models, which had been very small at first but took off by the late 'seventies.

Meanwhile, Leyland had been busy developing its own new coach chassis, aware of growing challenge from imported makes. The Leopard had gradually 'grown up' from its original 1959 concept and had a very good reputation on reliability but by 1980 was beginning to be left behind, literally and in specification, by some of its competitors. For several years around the mid-'seventies it was very much dependent on the NBC and SBG for sales, becoming the former's usual choice for coach duties usually with broadly similar Duple or Plaxton bodywork and the latter's most widely-used single-decker, very largely with Alexander Y-type body, often of the dual-purpose form much favoured in Scotland, though also including pure bus and coach versions.

However, the increase in weight

and inclusion of 12-metre versions in addition to the more usual 11- or less common 10-metre chassis had brought the 680 engine (the 11-litre version of the unit first seen in vertical form in what was then called O.600 9.8-litre form in the Titan PD2 of 1947) to a point where it was becoming underpowered with 175bhp as the maximum offered. There was also criticism of a harsh ride from the leaf springs and sometimes of high noise level, though so far as passengers were concerned, good body design could keep that under control.

Consultation with NBC, as the largest customer, on a new model, at first called B43, began in the mid-'seventies, though growing sales to independent operators and pressure from them through CPT led to the discussions being widened. There was also a change of mind in regard to suspension, which was originally planned as leaf-spring again, but with an air-suspension option. A combination of pressure for improvement and feedback of impressively good reliability with the Leyland National's air suspension from NBC operators led to air suspension being adopted as standard before the model was launched with Tiger name early in 1981. The TL11 engine, though of the same capacity as the 680 and derived from it, was turbocharged and put the initial power output up to 218

bhp, later increased further with a 245 bhp option and then again to 260 bhp by 1984. The driving position was also altered, falling into line with the Olympian and Leyland National to some degree with use of a more inclined steering column and smaller steering wheel.

For much of the 'seventies the Leopard had been available only with Pneumo-cyclic air-operated epicyclic Wilson-type gearbox, this having become standard for virtually all NBC orders for full-sized Leyland vehicles, though an exception was made for some time for the SBG group which preferred synchromesh. However, in 1979 a version with ZF six-speed synchromesh gearbox was added to the range, this tending to be favoured by independent operators, often users of the AEC Reliance with this box which ceased production that year (though a few examples from dealers' stocks continued to enter service until 1981). The Tiger offered either the ZF box or the Pneumocyclic.

Leopard production continued for a couple of years and the total delivered to British operators in 1981 was over 500, Tiger models not beginning to reach operators in any quantity until towards the end of the year. Even in 1982 the Leopard was still in front with 300 or so, though only marginally ahead of the Tiger but in 1983, Leyland was able to claim first place among single-

The Leyland Tiger, though shown in chassis form at the 1980 Show, identified at that stage merely as B43, was not officially launched until early 1981 and only limited numbers had reached operators' fleets before the end of the year. They tended to be regarded as rather special, with the Leopard soldiering on and often still outnumbering the new model among deliveries during 1982. Certainly in this category was Alexander (Northern) AFC1, delivered at the end of 1981 and given its own fleet number series to mark the fact that it was the Aberdeen Football Club team coach. The body was of the Duple Dominant III type with relatively shallow windows and forward-inclined pillars, which gave it an appearance reminiscent of the Alexander M-type motorway coaches built on various chassis for SBG between 1968 and 1976. Seating, with tables, was provided for only 29 passengers. It is seen at the St. Andrews Square bus station, Edinburgh.

The Leyland Tiger moved into first place among sales of single-deck models in 1983, half of the total of over 700 being coaches for NBC subsidiaries and accounting for most of that group's record intake of coaches that year. The vehicle shown, Maidstone & District 281 (A181 MKE) was one of ten with Duple Laser 53-seat bodywork placed in service towards the end of the year. It is seen on private hire duty in Skipton bus station in the summer of 1985. The Laser was one of two new Duple coach body designs introduced to replace the Dominant coach range at the 1982 Show, being readily identified by its strongly-raked windscreen.

deck models for the Tiger, with over 700 delivered, though there were still over a couple of dozen Leopards in that model's final year. The Tiger was still top in 1984 and 1985, though numbers went down below 500 due to the fall in the market as a whole.

Thus Leyland was in a strong position through the early 'eighties, even if its near-monopoly of bus sales of the mid-'seventies had gone. Its deliveries of buses and coaches to British operators outnumbered all other makes added together up to 1981 and only dipped marginally below this level up to 1983. However in 1982, NBC decided to pull out of the half share in Bus Manufacturers (Holdings) Ltd it held, selling its holding to Leyland Vehicles Ltd which held the other half. This was done because BM(H) had made a loss in 1981, NBC having to pay £1.1 million in consequence – the sharp drop in Leyland National sales was not only biting but the prospects were considered depressing.

This ended the direct association of major bus operating and manufacturing interests which could be traced back not only to the formation of Leyland National in 1969, Tilling's acquisition of the Bristol concern in 1931 and the group connection with the bodybuilding activities of United in 1929 (the latter later passing via Eastern Counties to ECW) but in principle going back to Tilling's involvement with the Tilling-Stevens firm on its formation in 1906.

In practical terms no immediate change in policy was discernible, for

NBC continued to place most of its orders with Leyland – some 265 of the record deliveries of 477 Olympians in 1983 were for NBC. The decision to close the factory of Bristol Commercial Vehicles Ltd at Brislington, Bristol, in 1983 was not directly related, though it did reflect surplus capacity within the Leyland group as a whole. The Bristol concern, originally the Bristol Tramways & Carriage Co Ltd, had made bus chassis, initially for its own use, since 1908, building up a reputation for rugged durability from soon after its vehicles were sold to a wider market in the 'twenties. The make name Bristol had all but disappeared, apart from the handful of late LHS chassis, but some 995 of the Leyland Olympian double-deck chassis were built by BCV up to September 1983.

Olympian chassis production was moved to Workington, helping to fill the gap by the drop in Leyland National business. By the end of 1985, a further 1000 chassis had been built, including a sizeable proportion of three-axle chassis for export to Hong Kong. Production of the Titan as a London-only vehicle was becoming increasingly uneconomic and Leyland had exerted strong pressure to increase its share of London orders. The 1981 split between Leyland for the Titan and MCW for the Metrobus was 150 and 300, the former being relatively low to allow for the transfer of production to Workington from Park Royal, which had finished after building the first 250 London Titans. For 1982, Leyland got the entire

order of 275, a decision which led to lay-offs at MCW. The 1983 order was 210 Titan and 150 Metrobus and the decision was then taken that a final batch of 240 Titans would be built, this being completed in October 1984, bringing the London total of this model to 1,125 – London orders for Metrobuses were for 150 and 335, for delivery in 1984 and 1985, making London's total of what was later called the Metrobus Mark I reach 1,440.

The thought of new double-deckers entering London service at an average rate of 362 per year – virtually one every day – over the 1981-85 period seems remote indeed a decade later, when manufacturers report a single London double-decker order for a tenth of that size with pride!

Before leaving the London bus supply story, it should be recorded that an Alternative Vehicle Evaluation programme led to the ordering of three each of Leyland Olympian, MCW Metrobus (two of a revised design with simplified body construction called Mark II, already adopted for non-London orders), Dennis Dominator and Volvo Ailsa B55, all being delivered in 1984-85. The third Metrobus was to be of a proposed Mark III version of advanced design, but MCW decided not to proceed with this in view of the uncertainty of London bus orders in the political climate of the time.

The main threat to Leyland was from the Swedish manufacturer Volvo, though any thought that Leyland Bus, as the passenger side of the business

This photograph of the first Leyland Olympian chassis to be completed at the Leyland Bus factory at Workington was issued to the press on 23rd August 1983, there being a slight overlap, as the last Bristol-built Olympian did not leave the Bristol Commercial Vehicles works until the following month. The accompanying press release did not indicate whether it was numerically the first of the new series, of which chassis numbers began at 1001; the Bristol-built series, which began at 1 ended at 995 (there was also the nine prototypes in a separate B45 series numbered 0 to 09). One of fifteen for Crosville, it had the Gardner 6LXB engine generally favoured for this model by NBC, and five-speed Hydracyclic gearbox with built-in retarder. In the background are three of the Titans then being built for London Transport, including T796 (OHV 796Y) nearest the camera.

London Transport's engineers were considering the possibilities for the next generation of London buses, and while in some respects moving further from the idea of a vehicle tailor-made to meet the special needs of the metropolis, the Alternative Vehicle Evaluation programme did pursue some quite radical ideas. In terms of layout, the most intriguing was the third of the Volvo Ailsa B55-10 Mark 3 buses, V3, seen here in September 1985, six months after entering service as the last of the AVE vehicles. Its Alexander bodywork took advantage of the front engine position to move the exit door from the usual centre position to the rear, adding a second staircase. Its seating capacity was thereby reduced to 64, reminiscent of a standard Routemaster, as compared to 76 for the two other Ailsa buses. The appearance of Volvo vehicles in what by then was the London Buses fleet aroused interest but at that stage there was little expectation that much more would be heard of Volvo in the mainstream of bus manufacture for Britain, despite its growing importance as a coach chassis maker, but later events were to alter matters radically.

had been named from 1981, would become a Volvo subsidiary, would have seemed incredible at that date, and even more so that it would close in 1992.

The mid-engined Volvo B58 had built up substantial sales as a coach chassis since its introduction to Britain in 1972, reaching just under 400, almost entirely with independent operators, by 1980.

That year, the new B10M chassis appeared at the Motor Show (as did Leyland's B43, yet to receive its Tiger name). It was a mid-engined model and continued many of the features of its predecessor, including the basic design of its Volvo 9.6-litre engine, turbocharged and producing 262 bhp. There was the ZF six-speed synchromesh gearbox, air suspension being standard, available at first only in 12-metre form. As with Leyland, the new model did not immediately

supersede the old and although total Volvo single-deck sales dropped below the 1980 figure during the following four years, the market share rose. Particularly significant was the way in which by 1982 the B10M was the most popular coach chassis in terms of individual models among sales to independent operators.

Taking the single-deck market as a whole, Volvo's sales were second only to Leyland from 1982 and the share of the total coach market in 1984 was almost a quarter, climbing steadily closer to Leyland's share, then running at a third of the total.

A third contender to do battle with the Tiger and B10M was the DAF MB200, again a mid-engined coach chassis. The DAF concern had begun making commercial vehicles in the post-war years, at first using Leyland engines but had graduated to developing its own engines, though still with

obvious Leyland design influence, by the 'sixties. This association was to prove ironic in view of the take-over of Leyland Truck by DAF in 1987. This Dutch concern was virtually unknown in the British coach business until 1978 when chassis began to be imported, a dozen being sold that year. By 1980, the figure had risen to 46, but the MB200, with 11.6-litre 252 bhp engine, moved into a bigger league by 1982 when nearly 150 were sold in Britain. By 1983, DAF had overtaken both Ford and Bedford in single-deck chassis sales, mainly on the strength of the MB200 with a total of 194, though about a quarter of these were of the rear-engined SB2300 type, a subject to be touched upon later.

During the early 'eighties I was road-testing a variety of coach models for *Coaching Journal* and the DAF MB200, Leyland Tiger and Volvo B10M all came my way in 1981-82.

They were quite evenly matched and all shared basically the same ZF six-speed gearbox in synchromesh form. The semi-automatic version of the Leyland, as favoured by NBC and by that date SBG, was by far the easiest to drive but lost out in hilly terrain because of the lack of the nicely-judged set of gear ratios towards the top of the range given by the ZF synchro box. The Volvo scored on overall engine smoothness and excellent power steering, the DAF had the easiest manual gearchange and good hilly-route performance while the Tiger seemed to have a particularly good blend of ride comfort and stability as well as plenty of low-speed torque.

The truth was that all three models offered very high standards and I was not convinced of the alleged overall advantages of rear-engined coach models, about which there was much talk but only limited sales support in Britain. Certainly, right up to the end of the period covered by this book, mid-engined models accounted for three-quarters of all coach sales, though it has to be conceded that this proportion had been about 98 per cent in 1980. The rise of interest in the rear-engined coach is examined later.

Within a few years, there had been quite a change in the many aspects of the coach scene. When London Country Bus Services Ltd began to replace most of the then existing Green Line fleet in the late 'seventies, the new vehicles with bodywork by Duple or Plaxton, basically of the standard designs of those two concerns, the new fleet seemed up-to-date and helped to lift the image of those services, but were not expected to be seen beyond the environs of London. Illustrated here is RS113, an AEC Reliance with Plaxton Supreme IV Express bodywork placed in service in the late summer of 1979, shortly after the AEC factory at Southall closed and production of the Reliance ceased. It is seen in June 1983 at Paignton on route 703 (London-Brixham) where the arrival of a Green Line coach so far from London on an express service would have been greeted with incredulity a few years earlier.

Perhaps most typical of the mid-'eighties coach was the Plaxton Paramount design, with its characteristic slope to the front third or so of the waistline. The NBC companies between them placed about 350 Plaxton-bodied coaches in service in the years 1983 and 1984, Midland Red (South) No. 2 (A191 GVC) seen here being typical, based on Leyland Tiger chassis and having 49-seat Paramount 3200 Express bodywork. It is shown leaving the small but strategically placed Wellington Street coach station in Leeds, bound for Glasgow in June 1984.

The MAN SR280 seemed to catch the imagination of British coach operators and although numbers sold were modest in relation to the overall market, it influenced the industry significantly. The rather severe lines were exploited effectively in this example of the Highliner version, A32 UDS, placed in service by Hutchison's Coaches (Overtown) Ltd, previously an AEC and then Volvo user. It is seen at Moffat, much favoured as a coach refreshment stop off the A74 road.

Chapter seven:
More rear engines ... or not?

From the late 'sixties, there had been a minority of imported bodywork, complete vehicles or, a little later, chassis to be found among the coaches placed in service by independent operators. In general, numbers were very small, the nearest approach to a serious breakthrough into this market up to the late 'seventies being that of Caetano bodywork, though later Van

The author at the wheel of a left-hand-drive MAN demonstrator. Effortless performance, and in particular ability to maintain speed on motorway gradients, was part of the appeal of the model.

Hool began to have a small but fairly steady following. Mercedes-Benz made several attempts to gain a foothold with its rear-engined integral coaches, but quantities were very limited, their high cost not being considered justifiable by most operators. Then Volvo began to establish a firmer position with the B58 chassis – a good performer, but on the whole, quite orthodox, imported in small numbers from 1972 but later making more serious inroads, sales rising to 98 in 1978 and 215 in 1979.

More dramatic was the appearance on the scene of MAN with its SR280 model, of which 24 were sold in Britain in 1980. This old-established concern –

Dr Rudolf Diesel built his first operational engine in its workshops – had been little-known in this country, though the arrival of a MAN right-hand-drive demonstrator articulated bus in Britain in 1978 followed by the entry into service of four more during South Yorkshire PTE's period of experimental running of such vehicles drew attention to its activities. The impact of the SR280 was of a model with a combination of high-specification features – 280 bhp rear-mounted 11.4-litre horizontal engine; integral construction; air suspension, independent at the front; toilet and driver's sleeping compartment.

Two dozen sales in a year may not seem very impressive at a time when the total coach market in Britain was nearly a hundred times as many, but it was quite an achievement when even the mighty Mercedes-Benz had been knocking at much the same door with little success in Britain for fifteen years or so. One factor may have been the timing, with strengthened interest in such vehicles for use on deregulated express services – significantly buyers included firms such as Park's and Trathen's, who were to be very active from October 1980. Another might well have been the agreeable personality of Richard Noy, in charge of MAN coach sales. In the following two years, sales rose slightly to 28 and then 30, but then fell off quite sharply, but the influence on the British industry was quite considerable.

Another strand to the interest in rear-engined integral coaches came from a small Dutch concern, Bova, whose modest but well-planned works was sited only a few kilometres from the DAF headquarters at Eindhoven. At that date there was no financial link between the two, but it was natural for DAF engines and other mechanical units to be used, though Bova did design its own front suspension, for example. This vehicle, type EL26, was pitched at a different market to the MAN, being lighter at just over 10 tonnes compared to 12 tonnes and using a DAF 8.27-litre engine and costing only relatively little more than, say, a Leyland Leopard Plaxton-bodied coach of the same 12-metre length.

Bova made Britain its main export target, and beginning with eighteen coaches sold here in 1981, sales rose to 92 and then 91 before dropping in 1984, though this was more than balanced by the development of a joint exercise with Duple, combining the Bova underframe with Duple bodywork as the Calypso. Meanwhile Bova had itself introduced a new model for the 1984

One of the leading Continental marques of integral coach that began to make an impact on the British market in the early 'eighties was Setra, the trade name for the integral coaches built by the Kässbohrer concern at Ulm in Germany. Pitched at the top end of the market, Setra coaches tend to be regarded as a long-term investment. When Charterplan, the coaching offshoot of Greater Manchester Transport, placed two Setra S215WD high-floor 49-seat models in service early in 1983, they were given registration numbers without date prefix letters previously carried by Guy Arab IV double-deckers dating from 1961-62 of Lancashire United Transport, taken over by GMT in 1976, the vehicles in question having been used for training latterly. Seen here bringing a touch of glamour to a Coronation Street-style setting are 515 VTB and 583 TD, respectively Nos. 30 and 31. The S215 was part of a range introduced in 1976 but its styling has proved to have a non-dating appeal.

season, the Futura, with a rather bulbous streamlined nose. Total all-Bova sales were 72 but the Duple-bodied version brought the total up to 108, though this dropped back to 52 in 1985.

Rear-engined coaches of other imported makes also began to make a showing on the British market. Notable amongst them were both of the two leading 'independent' makers in Germany – Auwärter and Kässbohrer, better known by their respective trading names Neoplan and Setra. Both were established builders of integral-construction coaches of advanced design, with independent front suspension and disc brakes, though using engines, gearboxes and some other items supplied by other concerns, mainly Mercedes-Benz. Neoplan was best known for its rather exotic-looking double-deck six-wheel Skyliner coaches, in production since 1968, but also building single-deckers, whereas the boot was rather on the other foot with Setra. Both firms appeared on the British market in 1981 with a handful of vehicles between them, but in 1982 began to make a significant showing, with 31 Setra single-deck coaches while Neoplan's showing was 14 double-deckers and 13 singles. Both firms continued at a fairly consistent level to 1984, though Setra also came into the double-deck coach picture, beginning with one vehicle in 1983 and rising to 19 in 1984 – Neoplan's double-deck deliveries that year rose to 26 – in both cases remarkable figures for what were very expensive vehicles. In 1985 there was a drop in figures, but this was partly a reflection of reduced overall demand.

Slightly ironically, Mercedes-

Benz's own rear-engined model, the O303 with integral construction and 14-litre V8 engine, available in Britain since soon after its introduction in 1973, finally began to make better progress in 1982, when 20 were sold here, followed by 26 the following year, probably thanks to livelier marketing by the Yeates dealer organisation.

Another way of tackling what was a growing, even if still minority, demand for rear-engined coaches was by supplying a form of 'chassis' which was designed to be split in two. This was the concept that had been used by Scania for its buses including the MCW-built Metro-Scania and Metropolitan of the 'seventies. The switch of MCW

Scania returned to the British bus market from 1980 with a model no longer tied to one bodybuilder, after the decision by MCW to build complete vehicles had ended the Metro-Scania and Metropolitan production runs. Two BR112DH demonstrators with East Lancashire bodywork of alternative 9.5 and 10-metre lengths were built in the autumn of 1980. The shorter of these was taken into stock by Nottingham City Transport the following spring and was placed in service with its largely blue livery taken as a basis for all-over advertisement for Scania and the Associated Saab cars in conjunction with a local dealership. Number 400 (NRR 400W) is seen here in April 1983 – a second later similar Scania demonstrator was also acquired, but Nottingham's rather limited orders for new buses in the period went elsewhere.

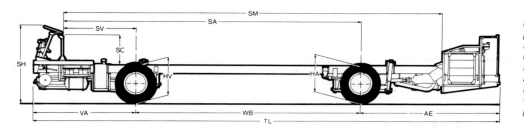

The DAF SB2300 rear-engined 12-metre coach chassis, like its very similar predecessor the SB2005, was designed so that the centre section of the chassis could be literally sawn away, after a suitable body had been mounted, to give an unobstructed luggage area below floor level. The centre section of the frame was kept as simple as possible, and all piping and wiring re-run to suit.

to an own-design underframe for the Metrobus ended that association and, for some years, Scania passenger vehicles did not figure in the British market, though its heavy goods representation remained strong. It reappeared at the 1980 Motor Show with an updated BR112-series model (later the designation became N112) using a conventional chassis with the Voith three-speed or Scania four-speed automatic transmission, the latter overcoming the main shortcoming of the Metropolitan. At first, interest was limited, with single examples with East Lancs body for Leicester and Nottingham and eleven with Marshall bodies for Newport (the latter having been the most consistent municipal user of Scania-based buses since the early days of the Metro-Scania single-decker). However, Scania broke into the coach market with a model using the 'split-chassis' concept familiar on buses of the earlier generation, the front and rear sub-frames, temporarily linked so that they could be driven to the bodybuilder and then spaced out to suit the body structure into which they were to be built.

The K112 coach with what was basically the familiar 11-litre engine but mounted longitudinally and turbocharged to give some 305 bhp appeared in Britain at the 1982 Show with a Jonckheere body – another name which had already made significant progress in Britain (its sales rising from a mere five in 1980 to 58 in 1981 and 90 in 1982, levelling off at 118 in both 1983 and 1984 before dropping to 78 in 1985). Total Scania sales remained more modest during that period, the double-decker barely breaking into double figures while the single-deck versions, which included a few buses for Newport, rose steadily if not dramatically from 29 to 52. A lighter coach version, the K92 with 8.5-litre engine was announced in 1984, but examples did not arrive on the British market until 1986.

Another way of achieving much the same idea was that offered by DAF which, on its rear-engined coach models, supplied a complete chassis but this was so designed that the centre section – simple straight framework – was intended to be cut away after the body was built on. Metal-framed coach bodywork of most types had adequate strength and rigidity to allow this to be done without more than minor revision, and models for such chassis had suitable framing for the underfloor luggage compartment, adding to the rigidity of the structure above. The first version offered was the SB2005, of which fifteen entered service in Britain in 1982. This was superseded by the SB2300, both having a smaller, 8.25-litre, engine than the mid-engined MB200, though the power output, up to 244 bhp, was not far behind, due to a combination of running up to a high speed and a fairly high degree of turbocharging. By 1984, DAF's coach sales in Britain of 140 chassis were split roughly equally between mid- and rear-engined models. At the Show that year, the new SB3000 added the 11.6-litre engine to the rear-engined range.

This build-up of interest in rear-engined coaches, quite often with advanced technical features, could fairly be described as at least partly bound up with the general growing trend towards higher-specification coaches – it was becoming more common to include toilet and refreshment facilities as well as such features as reclining seats among the features of coaches generally. However, there was also a practical factor which was of growing importance. Increased room for luggage was becoming more important, for tourists – notably from the United States or Japan – were apt to bring more luggage, quite apart from that of British holidaymakers bound for distant destinations. The between-axles space, particularly on a high-floor model, offered the possibility of providing more room than is available

in the rear overhang of a mid-engined model even if side lockers are also provided.

This factor, plus the more general one of high-spec coaches, was engaging the attention of both the operators who traditionally 'bought British' and their suppliers. Until around 1984, the idea of any of the publicly-owned operators buying significant numbers of imported vehicles was virtually ruled out, though that philosophy was being eroded by what were at first small batches for specialised purposes or evaluation.

In particular, NBC was very conscious of a need to be able to provide a higher standard of performance and comfort, partly to compete with a small number of operators who were already running coaches of high performance, high-specification type and partly to offer standards of travel comparable to railway services – understandably, British Rail was not taking the increased road competition lying down.

By the beginning of December 1981, NBC had decided to introduce what were to be called Rapide services the following spring. As an interim step, some standard Leyland Leopard coaches were to be equipped with hostess-service refreshment facilities, toilets and video units by Ribble at Preston and Midland Red at Carlyle Works, Birmingham. More significantly, there was an existing programme of developing a dual-purpose coach on rear-engined Dennis Falcon chassis with Gardner engine and Duple body.

Courageously, Dennis agreed to take on the job of developing a high-performance coach at a meeting on 23rd December 1981 and it was agreed that it should be based on the Falcon chassis but using the Perkins TV8/640 turbocharged V8 engine as the power unit available in the time-scale that would meet the performance requirement. It was to be coupled to Voith D854 four-speed automatic transmission. Duple was to develop a suitable body and again because of the time factor this was to be based on the existing high-floor Goldliner design, rather than a new design being developed for the 1982 Show. The first vehicle was due to enter service by 1st June.

At first, Dennis worked on a goodwill basis, developing the design and constructing ten chassis. The official order was not placed until early April 1982 yet by the end of that month all ten chassis were delivered to Duple. Construction of the bodies was also urgent but problems arose with video installations – at that date, no one, either among suppliers or operators, had any significant experience of such in coaches. Almost inevitably, completion was late, the first vehicle being delivered, to Western National, in September 1982 and the last just before the end of that year.

There had been no time for testing, and effectively they entered service straight off the drawing board. It was an almost hopelessly optimistic timetable, and it was hardly surprising that troubles began to be experienced. There was some lack of rigidity in the front of the body, causing the plug-type door to open at speed and hence the engine to be shut down via the safety interlock; a tendency to overheat; fuel leaks, and video equipment failures. It is rather sad that what was a promising design, with nothing fundamental wrong with it, should have earned a poor reputation that a few months of development work could have overcome – the fault, if any, was in attempting too much in too short a time-span. It is also worth setting the record straight by recording that some of the vehicles had covered over 200,000 miles within two years.

In general, Rapide and other NBC services were further developed using Leyland Tiger coaches of which some

The ten Dennis Falcon V coaches supplied to NBC subsidiaries for the new Rapide express services were an example of a promising design project let down by excessive pressure to get the vehicles into service before there had been time to carry out an adequate testing and development programme. For similar reasons, it was unfortunate that they had bodywork of Duple's Super Goldliner design, about to be superseded by the Caribbean. Seen here in March 1983 is National Travel West No. 99 (ANA 99Y), one of two coaches for that operator transferred to Southern National later in 1983.

350 were added to the Group's fleets in 1983 and it was fortuitous that both Duple and Plaxton had new-generation coaches introduced at the 1982 Show to replace the Dominant and Panorama Elite/Supreme styles that had been so familiar over the previous decade. The concept of using higher floor levels, partly to improve the view over the countryside but more as a means of increasing luggage space, was growing in popularity. Duple decided to separate the normal and high floor designs in terms of styling and the Laser was noteworthy in having a more raked windscreen than the higher-built Caribbean, the latter perhaps intended to emulate the rather severe lines of

many Continental designs. Plaxton's Paramount as introduced had a sloping waistline from windscreen level to the rear of the first main side window, at which point there was a small 'feature window'. It was built in normal and high form, distinguished by their approximate height in millimetres – 3200 and 3500. Examples of all entered NBC coach fleets with alternative interior layout to suit use on normal express, Rapide or holiday duties. Plaxton alone built about 230 coaches for NBC in 1983 and Duple nearly 100. Other types were used, also, notably Bova coaches for National Travel (London) and Berkhof bodywork both on DAF chassis and later the Leyland

The Plaxton Paramount body, mainly mounted on mid-engined chassis, had a big following after its introduction at the 1982 Show. The firm's output for 1983 was boosted by big NBC orders, but independent operators of all types formed the core of the business that resulted. Seen at Shap Wells in July 1985 are five examples of the Paramount 3500 high-floor version on Leyland Tiger chassis in service with the Shearings group, B508 UNB nearest the camera returning from a Scottish Lochs tour.

Eastern Coach Works returned to coach body manufacture after a long interval in 1982-83. The resulting vehicles were generally based on new Leyland chassis, but in this case on a reconditioned Leyland Leopard chassis dating from 1970, one of four for Midland Red (Coaches) Ltd in 1983. Number 549, re-registered as ROG 549Y in its rebuilt form, is seen in July 1985 on National Holidays duties in Inverary. The body design showed Leyland influence, the windscreen with black border below to increase its apparent depth being a feature of a new goods range of the time.

Tiger. In fact there was more variety in NBC's coach intake from 1982 onwards, with ECW and Alexander among other suppliers. ECW had not built coaches since the early 'seventies but supplied 151 in 1982-83. Sadly, and yet in a way also happening elsewhere within the Leyland group, ECW ran into problems. The rear-end structural design gave trouble and they had to be recalled for strengthening of the boot floor. It was very unlike ECW to make an error of such a kind.

However, the growth in the demand for coach services on some of the major trunk routes caused both NBC and SBG to be attracted by the idea of using double-deckers. Here again, the use of Neoplan double-deckers by such firms as Trathen's doubtless provided a spur, but the idea of buying foreign products, which would by their very nature have been prominent, would have been

embarrassing, to say the least, for a nationalised concern at that period. There was also some reluctance to accept the limited internal headroom dictated by the fact that such vehicles were built to the usual continental height limit of 4 metre (13ft. 1.5in.), not relevant in this context as it was not planned to use these vehicles outside Britain.

MCW realised it had the basis of a comparable 12-metre six-wheel double-deck coach in the Metrobus models of this size and configuration, sometimes called the Super Metrobus, and built primarily for Hong Kong. That model was built to 14ft. 8in. height, but it proved possible to get the coach version, known as the Metroliner, down to 13ft. 10.5in., about 9in. taller than the 4-metre limit, while giving adequate headroom in both decks – in other words, roughly similar to a typical

British low-height double-deck bus as widely specified by NBC. To give adequate performance the Cummins 10-litre L10 engine – itself newly-introduced in Britain and normally rated at 180 or 250 bhp for bus and coach work respectively, was incorporated and used in its high-rated 290 bhp form, this output being produced at a relatively modest 2,200 rpm. The transmission, as usual on MCW models, was a Voith fully-automatic but in this case a four-speed unit. Air suspension could be taken for granted by that date.

The Scottish Bus Group was first off the mark, in the sense that the first completed vehicle was in a version of SBG corporate coach livery when put on display at the Motor Show at the NEC in October 1982. However, NBC was involved in the early discussions on the possibilities, and by March 1983, a report had been prepared on the

The MCW Metroliner was an impressive vehicle, even in its 'basic' form, as used on non-Rapide services. The vehicle seen here in November 1984 was supplied to National Travel (West) Ltd but had passed to Ribble, retaining the same number 119, on 10th May 1984 as part of the process of dismantling the original National Travel fleets. In this form, the model seated 79 passengers as compared to 73 with refreshment and toilet facilities on the Rapide version.

possibilities of using double-deck coaches which was the basis of deciding on their adoption and the decision to order 39 of the type. The additional cost compared to 39 of the Tigers that would have been ordered was £1.7 million, but it was calculated that the additional revenue they would earn would recover this early in the fourth year of service.

Sixteen of the original NBC batch were to Rapide specification with 73 reclining seats, toilet, refreshment facilities etc, the remaining 23 being 79-seat coaches for normal express service. The prototype made an inaugural run from Glasgow to London in April 1983 but later that year was transferred to Alexander (Northern). The first of the NBC batch was delivered in April 1984, the remainder of the order following later in 1984. They were allocated to various subsidiaries, allocations being revised in some cases as a result of trade union problems. The Scottish Bus Group's first production batch of seven, seating 69 like the prototype, also entered service in 1984 and Tyne & Wear PTE put four, also 69-seat but to a different layout, into service on the Clipper service from Newcastle to London, bearing the Armstrong Galley livery of its coaching subsidiary. Various repeat orders, mainly for various NBC companies, followed. They were used intensively, many building up mileages of around 200,000 per year and over 100 were in service by the end of 1985 – ultimately, 127 of the Cummins L10 powered Metroliner six-wheel double-deckers were built by the time production ceased in 1986.

Mention should also be made of the single-deck Metroliner, the prototype of which was also at the 1982 Show. This was a rather plain-looking coach of 3.2-metre height, based on a separate chassis built, like those of the double-deckers, in MCW's own workshops. It, too, had the Cummins L10 engine, mounted longitudinally at the rear, with ZF synchromesh gearbox. Only 21 were built, the first of five for East Kent, in National Holidays livery being the Show exhibit, and being followed by six of the ten of an improved Mark II type included in this total.

A year later, the Metro-Hiliner appeared, this being a high-floor, single-deck coach. It differed from the other Metroliners in being a true integral and also had a less severe appearance – mechanically it was much the same as the previous single-deck version. This also met with very limited success, the eventual total built again being 21, though the last were not completed until 1987. As with the double-decker,

Less well-known were MCW's single-deck Metroliner coaches, of which the rather awkwardly-named Metro-Hiliner was noteworthy, not only for its high floor level but also because, unlike other MCW vehicles of the period, it was a true integral rather than having a chassis-like underframe. Among the small number of users was Premier Travel, of Cambridge, an old-established independent concern which had been one of the few to participate in joint operation with the State-owned NBC group and its predecessors before the deregulation of express services in 1980. Seen here in York in May 1985 is B192 JVA.

NBC and SBG companies accounted for most of both types, though Premier Travel of Cambridge took four of the Hiliner version.

Meanwhile, Leyland had been busy in similar sectors of the coach market. The coach version of the Olympian double-decker was less dramatic in effect than MCW's, being an 11-metre variant, retaining the standard model's basic mechanical design but with a 245 bhp version of the Leyland TL11 engine. The ECW body was also derived from the standard shell, but a surprisingly different appearance resulted from the use of deeper and quite sharply-raked upper-deck windscreen glasses. Its main function proved to be on commuter coach services into London on routes

from surrounding areas – a prototype for National Travel (West) appeared late in 1982, followed by five each for Maidstone & District and Alder Valley. Two more for the last-mentioned and five for London Country followed in 1984. Later that year, an improved version with smoother outline and rear-mounted staircase was developed and an example for Ebdons Coaches displayed at the Show.

A more ambitious project was the new-generation Royal Tiger. Leyland's first production underfloor-engined model of 1950-55 had used that name, but the revival of Tiger for the model of similar layout introduced in 1981 doubtless made Royal Tiger seem an appropriate name for an upmarket rear-

Leyland's offering as a double-deck coach was much more obviously a derivation of a standard product. The Leyland Olympian was provided with an ECW body given a 'different' look by the style of upper-deck windscreen. Seen here is the prototype, ADO 50Y, built for National Travel (West) in 1982 but carrying a Wessex fleetname in this 1983 photograph – it was transferred to the re-formed Wessex National Ltd in May 1984.

engined coach using generally similar mechanical units. The project had begun as B50, relating to the underframe, in 1980 and had been followed by B54 relating to a body design to be based on it. In a curious way, it was released a few weeks after the 1982 Show, and though a very impressive vehicle, in my view fully comparable to its Continental competitors, that odd timing was an unfortunate start and one that was sadly typical of the Leyland group at the time, and only the beginning of a troubled career.

Though clearly related to the Tiger, the Royal Tiger underframe was quite different in several respects. It was of space-frame construction, the front suspension was akin to that of the Olympian with air bellows set widely spaced to give good roll-resistance and the weight distribution was aided by mounting the fuel tank over the front axle. The horizontal 245 bhp TL11 engine and Hydracyclic gearbox were standard. The full title of the vehicle with standard body was to be Royal Tiger Doyen, though Leyland itself was not always consistent on this. Obviously the aim was to sell the vehicle in complete form, but Royal Tiger underframes were also married to other maker's body shells, notably Plaxton and Van Hool. The stylish standard body incorporated a contoured windscreen, the considerable depth of which was made to seem more by a black-painted area below it. The 3.4-metre height allowed the spacious luggage area below floor level expected

of the type and the neatly-finished interior was in the 'air-liner' style with enclosed lockers then just beginning to come into favour.

Special production facilities, including elaborate jigs for the welded underframe, were laid down at the factory of Charles H. Roe Ltd. Initial orders for the new model were quite encouraging – ten (later increased to 30) for NBC, six for SBG, four for Grey Green plus smaller numbers for other independent operators. Output was

depressingly slow, however, partly because of problems with the welded structure and partly because Roe, despite its excellent reputation as a bus bodybuilder, was not used to the complex individual variations for coach production for numerous customers, tending to delay production. Only eleven reached operators during 1983.

A second production facility, initially for the underframe, was set up at Workington towards the end of 1983 to deal with orders with other bodywork.

After the wave of interest in rear-engined coaches and the Dennis Falcon V vehicles for the NBC's Rapide services in particular, the appearance of the Dennis Dorchester was a rather unexpected return to tradition. Mid-engined and employing the Gardner power unit, it was intended to appeal to the Scottish Bus Group which had taken large numbers of Seddon vehicles based on much the same formula. However, this time, for coach applications the engine was the turbocharged 6HLXCT and air suspension was standard, so it also had up-to-date performance and comfort. Western SMT's N152, one of eight with Plaxton Paramount 3200 bodywork seating 49 placed in service in 1983, is seen at Anderston bus station, Glasgow, on the X22 Cityliner service to Wemyss Bay, a forerunner of the Scottish Citylink series of services. It is noteworthy that very briefly at the time of the 1982 Show this model was called the Lance, another old Dennis name, later revived for a quite different rear-engined single-decker.

For a while during the early 'eighties, it seemed as if Dennis would build vehicles in almost unlimited variety. The Dennis stand at the 1982 Show, as well as showing both Falcon V and Dorchester coach and Dominator bus chassis, included the first Falcon V double-decker, one of two for Nottingham – like the single-deck Falcon V, it had a rear-mounted vee-form engine but in this case a Mercedes-Benz OM421 V6 unit driving through a Voith D851 automatic gearbox. The East Lancs body, 34ft. 7in. (10.5-metre) long, seated 88, with 51 on the top deck, yet the unladen weight at 9.9 tonnes was no more than many 9.5-metre double-deckers. The appearance was based on the usual Nottingham outline, made even more unconventional at the time by the use of bonded windows with the angular look they tend to imply. The vehicle shown, No. 397 (XRA 397Y), was the second example, delivered early in 1983, and seen in service in April of that year.

Soon afterwards it was announced that volume production of the complete vehicle with Doyen body would also be switched, leaving Roe to deal with the smaller individual orders. Then, in May 1984 it was announced that the Roe works was to close in September and hence all Royal Tiger work would move to Workington. This further disruption did nothing to build up confidence and coach operators, to whom prompt delivery is tied to seasonal demand, were further discouraged from placing orders. Thus another promising British design was brought down by events.

The idea that British coach operators would follow their Continental equivalents in adopting rear-engined models to a much greater degree was not working out to the extent some expected. There was a

reaction in that mid-engined models began to fight back in one way and another. Perhaps one of the most important was the discovery that the Volvo B10M's frame design, built as low as possible, partly because of greater interest in the use of the model as a bus in its home market in Sweden and Scandinavia generally, also meant that it was possible to include a shallow but extensive luggage carrying area between the top of the chassis frame and the underside of the floor especially on high-floor coaches. Taken in combination with the rear locker, the B10M could give rear-engined models a run for their money in this important respect.

New mid-engined models continued to appear. Significantly, Dennis introduced the Dorchester chassis, with

engine amidships, at the 1982 Show, even though the first Falcon rear-engined coaches for NBC had only just entered service. It had the Gardner engine and ZF synchromesh gearbox as standard, in either the quite new 6HLXCT turbocharged 230 bhp or, for bus work, the more familiar 6HLXB 180 bhp form. At the demonstrations arranged in various parts of the country, the appearance of a Plaxton-bodied example, one of eight for Western SMT gave an indication of the market the manufacturers had particularly in mind. Central SMT took five buses, followed by ten coaches the following year. A few were sold to independents and municipalities but Leyland, in effect, shot Dennis's fox by introducing a Gardner-engined version of the Tiger towards the end of 1983. This, again,

was influenced by SBG and involved the same choice of engine – for 1984, the Group's order for Tigers was split between Gardner and Leyland-engined versions.

Bedford, after many years of sticking cautiously to building nothing longer than 11-metre models and to conventional leaf-spring suspension, made a belated move into the 12-metre air-suspension world at the 1984 Show. The new model, designated YNV and departing from previous practice by having a model name, Venturer, had the 8.2-litre engine as used previously but in the 205 bhp turbocharged form already offered on the YNT 11-metre chassis offered since 1982 (of which a few had been extended to 12-metre length before bodying). The gearbox was a ZF six-speed synchromesh unit. Had it been introduced a few years earlier, the Venturer might have arrested the slide in Bedford's coach sales figures, for it offered many of the attributes of dearer models at a very competitive price. With a depressed coach market, all that could be achieved was virtually constant annual sales of Bedford passenger chassis of all types at around 175 over the 1983-85 period, a mere shadow of the average of about 900 during the 'seventies. Ford, with no new

The Bedford YNV chassis was worlds away from the simple lightweight construction of early models of that marque and might have sold well had it been introduced in say 1980 rather than 1984. The choice of the model name Venturer doubtless seemed logical in use of a V initial as often found in Vauxhall cars (and Duple coach bodies for Bedford chassis) but, probably quite accidentally, revived a name once used for Albion double-deckers.

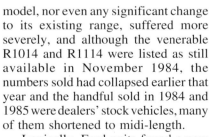

model, nor even any significant change to its existing range, suffered more severely, and although the venerable R1014 and R1114 were listed as still available in November 1984, the numbers sold had collapsed earlier that year and the handful sold in 1984 and 1985 were dealers' stock vehicles, many of them shortened to midi-length.

Ironically, Ford units found a new outlet, albeit briefly, in the products of Quest 80 Ltd, a small concern founded by R. T. (Dick) Knowles, a former AEC employee who was intrigued by the side-engined Q model, building a few chassis of similar layout for export. In 1984, a batch of twenty rear-engined

The anonymity of modern coach chassis, hidden almost completely by the bodywork, has often left the casual onlooker in doubt, but few might have been expected to recognise this vehicle as being a Quest model VM, using a chassis based on Ford Cargo components but with rear-mounted Ford 6-litre engine turbocharged and intercooled to give a remarkable output of 220 bhp by a concern specialising in power boat engines. Standing in front of one of 20 such vehicles are Vernon Maitland, Managing Director of Excelsior Holidays Ltd of Bournemouth, and, in the light suit, Dick Knowles of Quest 80 Ltd, at that date based in Telford. The Plaxton Paramount 3200 body had a deeper than standard windscreen to suit the low driving position of the chassis.

A noteworthy venture by a small operator was the construction of its own make of chassis. Ward Bros (Lepton) Ltd, with a fleet of eight coaches based near Huddersfield, decided on this course of action, using a Perkins engine, the initial vehicle, complete with Plaxton Supreme IV body, being seen here in June 1981. Further chassis of other operators followed and quite a good reputation was built up, needlessly dented, in the author's view, by the confusing choice of the names AEC and Albion with historic but quite unconnected connotations in a later reconstruction of the business.

models with Ford engines was built for Excelsior of Bournemouth. This was not the only manufacturing venture by a new small concern. Ward of Huddersfield, previously a coach operator, built six rear-engined bus chassis for Darlington and ten coach chassis with Perkins engines amidships for independent operators in 1983-84. The business ran into financial trouble despite quite well-thought out design but was reconstituted under the confusing title Albion Equipment Co Ltd (giving the initials 'AEC') by early 1985.

The original Albion concern, Albion Motors Ltd, of Scotstoun, Glasgow,

had been part of the Leyland group since 1951. Building of passenger chassis for the British market ceased in the 'sixties but exports had continued until 1980, when it was decided to transfer production to the Bathgate plant originally brought into the Leyland empire with the merger with the BMC group in 1968. Even though the Albion works thus closed, some passenger models of Albion origin were still being made for export, even though generally sold under the Leyland name. Also built at Bathgate was the Leyland Cub, a model introduced at the 1979 Show based on the Leyland Terrier goods chassis with 5.7-litre six-cylinder

engine, but with front axle set back and designed for bodywork in the 25-35 seat range according to wheelbase. Perhaps the most notable order was one for Lothian Regional Transport for eighteen examples in 1981 with automatic transmission and Duple bus bodywork. However, the Bathgate plant was itself closed under the same cutback in 1984 that brought the Roe concern to an end.

The demise of Roe was another step in the dismantling of the bus and coach manufacturing industry. It had never been a large concern but was widely respected. The days when it was a decidedly individualistic company

reflecting the ideas of Charles H. Roe, its founder, had ended with the cessation of teak-framed body construction in 1968, but it continued to have a good name, latterly closely tied into the Leyland organisation. Yet the closure of the works at Crossgates, on the outskirts of Leeds, was fiercely resisted locally, leading to the setting up, initially with financial assistance from the West Yorkshire Metropolitan County Council, of the independent Optare concern to continue bus body-building in the same premises, reopening in 1985.

Fresh ideas were not confined to the coach side of the business. Some 'new' ideas are really old ones transplanted into new soil, sometimes doing better than previously, sometimes not. One that recurs is the desirability of using chassis or units of basically unchanged form for widely different purposes. In the period up to about 1950-52, double- and single-deck bus and the larger coach chassis were often basically the same, with no more than minor differences in such matters as frame thickness, wheelbase, springs, tyre sizes and axle ratio differences. From time to time the idea of that concept has been revived. The rear-engined Dennis Falcon was one such, more especially in the version with a vee-form engine, and one of a pair with a Mercedes-Benz V8 and East Lancashire 88-seat body for Nottingham City Transport was exhibited at the 1982 Motor Show, as shown on page 69. Greater Manchester Transport took delivery of three Falcon double-deckers in its ongoing programme of buying small numbers of new or significant vehicles types (which also included pairs of Dennis Dominator, Volvo Ailsa B55 and Scania N112DH around the 1982-84 period).

However, a different approach was represented by another model, which was on display for the first time at that same 1982 Show. This was the Volvo Citybus, type B10MD. As the model number indicates, this was derived from the B10M with basically the same 9.6-litre THD100 engine mounted amidships. The concept of the original version was of a design largely resembling that of the front-engined B55 in that it was basically flat-topped but had the perimeter with squared-up sections over the axles designed to be directly attached to the body structure. A choice of Self-Changing Gears, Voith or ZF automatic transmission was offered. Versions to suit 10- or 11-

metre bodywork were offered and there was also a 12-metre three-axle version with steerable rearmost axle, also used on an Ailsa variant intended for the same Hong Kong market. A prototype with Marshall bodywork was already in service with Strathclyde PTE.

The idea of an underfloor-engined double-decker was not new, noteworthy British predecessors being the solitary AEC Regent IV (a double-deck version of the Regal IV) of 1949 and the two BMMO (Midland Red) D10 double-deckers of 1960-61. The former offered little if any practical advantage over the front-engined models of its day, the full-width cab being directly over the front axle. Midland Red did not take the idea beyond the pair of prototypes, but Volvo showed that the idea had many merits, being fortunate in that its dry-sump engine was particularly shallow. This was one of a number of design features that Volvo's underfloor-engined B58 and B10M shared with the AEC Regal IV – even their 9.6-litre engine size is reminiscent, though its bore and stroke and many other features are different. The frame height over the engine area (over which the floor panels could be laid directly) of the B10MD was 817mm (just over 2ft. 8in.), the floor thus a little over 4in. higher than the typical 2ft. 4in. of a normal-height rear-engined double-decker. Overall height of the prototype was 14ft.7in., an inch over the standard 14ft. 6in., though the ability to get down to the latter while maintaining saloon height legal requirements was claimed in the original literature.

There was considerable interest in the design, even though the front-engined Ailsa B55 continued in production – some 900 had been sold by the end of 1982. Citybus sales were cautious – in 1983 three were supplied to Derby and two to Nottingham, but in 1984 a broader spread of orders was achieved from PTE, municipal and SBG fleets resulting in a total of 29. By that date, the Ailsa was being phased out and the Citybus, for a time known as the D10M but nowadays again publicised as the B10M Citybus, grew further in popularity. The original concept altered and later versions are closer to the single-deck B10M in frame design.

Another new Volvo model appeared at the 1984 Show, this being the C10M integral coach, based on a stainless-steel space frame. Significantly, Volvo did not adopt the rear engine position for this, which could be described as an answer to the Royal Tiger. The engine was moved rearwards from its position on the B10M, leaving space for a full-depth luggage locker in the front half of

the between-axle space, but was still ahead of the rear axle. Also that year, the B9M shorter version of the B10M chassis appeared.

That 1984 Show had several noteworthy new models, despite the depressed state of the market – home-market sales of full-sized vehicles of all types to all types of operator were to be down to 2,438 the following year, under half what they had been in 1979. The first large-scale deliveries of minibuses increased that total to perhaps 3,000, as explained in the next chapter, but there was widespread concern at the prospects.

One of the most significant newcomers was the Leyland Lynx rear-engined single-decker seen in chassis form – the body structure design had yet to be completed. This had been Leyland project number B60, and although it was then stated that production of the Leyland National would continue, it was clear it was to be its successor. In one sense, this was a retreat from the National's concept as a

Although not put into production until the latter half of the 'eighties, the Leyland Lynx made its first public appearance at the 1984 Motor Show, in chassis form. In terms of manufacturing methods, it represented a step back from the extensive use of steel pressings with careful attention to rust prevention in the Leyland National. The distinctive body design attracted widespread approval in a visual sense after the rather 'stodgy' look of the National but in terms of durability the form of construction may not have represented an advance – perhaps a sign of the times. This example for the Nottingham City Transport fleet 1989 example showed evidence of Volvo influence in the rectangular radiator grille – Leyland having become a Volvo subsidiary the previous year.

A curious project was the so-called 'heavy-duty midibus' introduced by Leyland at the time of the 1984 Show and reviving another model name with echoes of the past – Tiger Cub. It was derived from a design developed by Leyland's subsidiary in Denmark, DAB, though the plan was for the vehicles to be finished by ECW. Its existence may have been influenced by NBC's swing away from lightweight models and in particular the Bristol LH, but carried the idea of something more substantial and better finished so far that it was more directly equivalent to a short version of the Tiger. United Automobile Services Ltd took delivery of the Show exhibit, numbering it 1500, in a series used for the LH, and allocated it to Richmond garage the following winter to operate on rural services as seen here, but it remained unique.

true 'pressed-steel' bus, made to some degree in the same way as modern cars, in favour of the traditional bus concept of a chassis (even if designed as the underframe of an integral), body framework plus panels. However, it was a promising design, with something of the flexibility of specification of the Olympian – alternative lengths between 10.4 and 12 metres were planned. The original engine options were Leyland TL11 or Gardner 6HLXCT horizontal units, with Hydracyclic transmission.

Virtually doomed from the start was a model described as a 'heavy-duty midibus', based on a Leyland DAB design which was to be imported from the DAB factory in shell form for finishing at ECW. It was to be either 9.5 or 10-metres long, with seats for up to 43 or 47 respectively, with the TL11 engine, Hydracyclic or Pneumatic transmission and taper-leaf springs. It was given the name Tiger Cub and a prototype was operated by United Automobile Services Ltd but with an unladen weight of about 8.5 tonnes, it was far removed from the realm of its namesake of the mid-'fifties, which weighed about 5.75 tons (the difference between the metric tonne and the

traditional British ton is very slight, so the numerical comparison is valid), still less that of a midibus of that period.

New Gardner engines have always been significant and there were three at the 1984 Show – at that stage the family firm had been taken into the Hawker-Siddeley empire. Perhaps most fascinating to people who remembered the many buses of the 'thirties, 'forties and 'fifties that had been powered by the 5LW five-cylinder unit was the 5LXCT, again of this layout and much the same in external size, of 8.7-litre capacity, and roughly twice as powerful at 170-185bhp. It was to be offered in Leyland, MCW and Dennis double-deckers but the subsequent collapse in the market killed the project. A new 6LXDT of 12.7-litres and developing up to 270bhp represented just about the maximum capability of the 6LX series – more recently it has been developed as the LG1200, now arousing special interest as a 'green' engine meeting the latest emission standards. Last but not least, there was the 6LYT, a completely new 15.5-litre unit developing up to 320 bhp – though meant for the articulated goods vehicle market mainly, it found an application in the

Neoplan six-wheel double-decker – the first example, for Harry Shaw of Coventry, was at the Show. I heard subsequently that its typically Gardner efficiency impressed some of the Mercedes-Benz engineers, but events over the following years did not allow that potential to be developed.

A last-minute addition to the 1984 Show was Duple's 425 integral coach. This superseded the earlier link with Bova and was an early consequence of Duple's absorption into the Hestair group which by then also owned Dennis. The Duple venture was independent of Dennis, though some of the latter's expertise was sought on aspects of the chassis design. Apart from an eye-catching outline – the name related to the drag coefficient of 0.425, claimed to be the industry's best – it used the Cummins L10 engine mounted at the rear and a particular point was made of weight reduction as well as the capability of high seating capacity. As shown, the vehicle was not fully developed and production did not begin in time for the 1985 season.

The Duple Integral 425 first appeared at the 1984 Motor Show and, though impressive-looking, needed further development and thus did not go into production immediately. It featured an unusual frontal profile, with the main part of the windscreen almost upright but the upper portion swept back quite sharply. By that date, Duple had come into the Hestair group of companies, as had Dennis, and although for a time both concerns were required to refer to themselves as Hestair-Duple and Hestair-Dennis respectively, these rather cumbersome names were never adopted generally.

Chapter Eight:
Minibus magic?

One of many reversals of previous thinking that arose in the mid-'eighties was the sudden large-scale adoption of the minibus. The idea that small buses might be the answer to some of the industry's problems was not new. Buses seating 20 or less had been commonplace in the 'twenties and 'thirties, generally being confined to rural routes. Apart from matching vehicle size to thinly-populated routes, they had the advantage that they could be operated without a conductor, not then permissible on larger buses.

Even so, the provision of services in such areas steadily became even more difficult as numbers of passengers fell further due to wider use of cars, and costs tended to rise. Very few buses seating less than 26 were built in the post-war years. However, concessions in the laws governing the constructional requirements on small-capacity vehicles were introduced in 1958 expressly to allow mass-produced van models to run as Public Service Vehicles (PSVs) – another of those rather misleading phrases that was still part of

the bus industry's everyday language. In practice, though such minibuses, as they were called almost immediately, were considerably cheaper than previous types of very small bus, the number of bus services run by them remained small. Those built were often used for contract or private hire work. This was partly because the major operating cost was the driver's pay, and certainly in large organisations with trade union agreements any idea that minibus drivers got mini wages was fiercely resisted.

Also, until 1965, the only van models on the market in Britain were too small to permit more than about eleven fare-paying passengers to be carried. The introduction of the Ford Transit, and in particular the 'parcel van' version which gave a 16-seat capacity as converted, as well as allowing something nearer to normal bus standards of entry, altered the situation and from about 1970 Mercedes-Benz, with a slightly larger pressed-steel van range, began to come into the picture, though at first only on

a very limited scale, and more often as a small coach.

Even so, the development of services using any kind of minibus was still very limited in the 'seventies. The driver's pay problem was occasionally by-passed by the idea of community buses, with unpaid volunteer drivers, and county council subsidy did allow some rural services to be run, though quite often operators found it better to run a somewhat larger type of bus which could take its turn on other duties. Such services were, by their nature, infrequent, and even when small buses were used for specialised suburban routes, say where there were narrow housing estate roads or other obstructions to the use of big buses, only handfuls of such vehicles were used.

Until the mid-'eighties, the typical bus fleet would include maybe a dozen or even fewer minibuses in a total strength of perhaps 250 or 500 or more vehicles. It was the Devon General experiment in Exeter beginning in the spring of 1984 and NBC's decision,

Until 1984, minibuses were only to be found in very limited numbers in major British bus fleets. Almost always they were used for small-scale operations needing only one or two vehicles. At the beginning of that year, City of Oxford Motor Services Ltd had just taken delivery of this Ford Transit with Dormobile 16-seat conversion of the standard 'parcel van' body for use as the Jericho Community Bus, for which purpose it was allocated to Chipping Norton garage and, as usual at that stage, given South Midland fleetnames as one of this concern's country-area vehicles. Although the Oxford company had been involved in earlier minibus experiments, there were at the time only two minibuses in the fleet of about 220 vehicles, quite typical of an NBC subsidiary at the time. South Midland became a separate company in June 1984.

industry is divided about the answer to that question. Clearly deregulation did alter the picture in the sense that an operator running comparatively big buses not very frequently, in order to keep the cost of operation in the off-peak period down to a level that was acceptable, was vulnerable to a competitor running a more frequent service. If frequency was the name of the game, then little buses were a cheaper way of providing it. It was also argued – and in some cases confirmed in practice – that more frequent buses generated more custom, so raising revenue and helping to pay the greater number of drivers needed. Another factor was that minibuses, more nimble than their larger brethren, could operate at a faster speed, helping to provide the required frequency at less cost than calculated on a straight comparison of numbers of vehicles operating at unchanged speeds passing a given point in a given time.

All the above is true to at least some degree, yet the basic facts, that the main cost in any bus operation is that of the man-power to run it and that a big vehicle's overall running costs do not go up in proportion to its size, remain. Exactly the same argument that makes the jumbo-jet the most economical machine for an airline to fly, provided it can be filled, applies to buses.

Another attitude to the minibus, as judged in the atmosphere of 1984-85, was perhaps rather more cynical. Those in the industry with a knowledge of history were aware of the use of small nimble buses as what were called 'chasers' in the period before the Road Traffic Act 1930. Little buses drew custom from a competitor's service by

confirmed by that exercise, to go in for minibuses on a much larger scale as a means of reacting to bus deregulation, that completely altered the picture. Inevitably other types of operator followed suit, though on the whole the local authority and PTE fleets were less enthusiastic. Some existing independent operators took up the idea on a modest scale and at one time it seemed likely that schemes akin to the AMOS proposal for London (itself at least partially the

trigger for NBC, even though it never came to fruition) might spring up with organisations like British Electric Traction making a reappearance in its old role of proprietor of a chain of bus operations, in various parts of Britain, but none got very far along that road.

What was the basis of this reversal of previous attitudes? If minibuses were simply uneconomic on a basis of cost per passenger mile before 1984-85, why was this no longer so? Even today , the

Following NBC's decision to adopt minibuses in a big way, facilities for the conversion of vans in large numbers were set up at both Carlyle Works in Birmingham (left), which had been the main works of the old Midland Red company, and the works of PMT at Stoke-on-Trent (right). The Ford Transit and the Mercedes-Benz L608D were the two main types of vehicle chosen for the

conversions, examples of both being visible in these two photographs. Carlyle Works, with a proud history of building vehicles of very advanced design, was set up as a separate company but what had become known as PMT Engineering remained part of the PMT operating company.

The Mercedes-Benz L608D was favoured to a growing extent as the NBC minibus programme expanded. Seen here is the first of a fleet of 39 with the van bodywork converted to 20-seat minibus form by Rootes of Maidstone, a factory whose origins could be traced to the Tilling-Stevens concern that supplied buses to many Tilling-associated companies in the period up to about 1930. Numbered 1001, it dated from the beginning of 1986. The livery was quite unusual at that date in retaining horizontal motifs which complemented the natural lines of the vehicle and not, as so often seemed the case, appearing to apologise for being a bus. The company fleetname was preferred to the fashionable childish slogans and the NBC double-N symbol was incorporated – new designs had been tending to drop it as privatisation approached – Maidstone & District was to be the sixth company to be sold off, in this case to a management team, in November 1986.

running just in front of the opposition's vehicle, relying on acceleration to overtake if passed while loading passengers. Independent operators using relatively lively, often American, small buses could out-perform the big operators' slower buses, quite often in those days based on 1914-18 war military chassis chosen for reliability rather than speed (theoretically limited by law to very slow speeds of 12 mph and later 20 mph, though these were widely ignored). Some of the big firms had fought back by buying their own small buses, the true chasers, to beat the opposition at its own game, and this thought was certainly in mind among some managers of major operators. On this basis the minibus would be merely a passing phase.

Another element in such thinking was the question of driver's wages. While operators held virtually monopoly powers over the bus routes for which they held licences, the trade unions had a correspondingly strong hold over the wages and conditions of bus crews. The Transport & General Workers' Union in particular, as well as covering most of the bus industry, had fought any development which it saw as a threat to its members' interests. It can be argued that its attitude was quite often self-defeating, as when prolonged strikes, especially in London, did permanent damage to the numbers of passengers, yet the general principle

is self-evident.

When minibus drivers were paid virtually the same as drivers of larger buses, as the unions tried to insist, the dice were loaded against widespread use of small vehicles. But under the pressure of heavy unemployment as experienced in the early 'eighties, a more flexible attitude had been forced on the unions. Among employers, themselves under pressure in a time of depression, there were some at least who saw the whole deregulation process and the use of minibuses in particular as a way of breaking the unions. The Government did not go so far as to express the idea publicly, but there were certainly some in high places who shared that thought. From this viewpoint, too, the large-scale use of the minibus was likely to be a passing phase rather than a permanency.

The story of how it all worked out belongs to the next volume in this series, rather than this one, but in the 1984-85 period there was a sharp upsurge in minibus orders. This was almost entirely due to NBC, and had that organisation not decided to take up the idea, it is a matter for conjecture as to whether the minibus 'explosion' would ever have happened. Modest numbers of 16-seat conversions of Ford Transit parcel-van models had been carried out by various firms since the late 'sixties, examples being distributed in small groups, quite often single

vehicles or pairs, in various parts of the country and owned by operators of various sorts. A few operators had slightly larger fleets, notably the 20 of London Transport dating from 1972-73 – five more had been added in 1979.

The total public sector (ie London Transport, PTE, municipalities, NBC and SBG) intake of such vehicles in 1983 was 22, of which NBC had eight. The Devon General experiment in Exeter plus other early exercises put NBC's intake of such vehicles up to 65 in 1984, yet other public sector operators took a mere eighteen. The 1985 figures were even more striking, comprising 485 for NBC and 23 for other public sector fleets. The intake of Ford Transit models to such organisations went up from three in 1983 to 47 in 1984 and 401 in 1985, the corresponding figures for Mercedes-Benz being six, 22 and 93.

Even more were to follow and visiting any of the works where the conversion work was going on was an odd experience at that time. The old Midland Red headquarters, at 1 Vernon Road, Edgbaston, was in front of what had long been called Carlyle Works, where in earlier days BMMO vehicles and earlier still SOS chassis had been made as well as overhauled. With the winding down of bus fleets and the reduced need for overhauls, partly due to design changes and partly the scrapping of the old system when it was normal for a vehicle due for re-certification (renewal of the Certificate of Fitness) after seven years' service or later to be given a thorough overhaul, such premises were short of work – particularly so at Carlyle with the ending of bus manufacture. Many had begun to take in outside work, but with the urgent need for minibuses, NBC fed a sizeable proportion of its needs through both Carlyle Works and also the PMT workshops, both thereby beginning new careers as minibus convertors and later builders of bodywork for the smaller sizes of bus.

In the vast yard at Carlyle in 1984-85 were possibly 100 or more Ford Transits, some in parcel-van form as supplied and others complete with seats and windows, ready for delivery. The conversion can only be described as very basic, and it seemed quite a come-down when compared to the impressive vehicles, often representing more advanced engineering than being offered by so-called professional manufacturers, in earlier decades.

The expectation that the public would take to the minibus as a more 'user-friendly' type of vehicle than the allegedly 'lumbering' full-sized bus was true up to a point. Certainly the general rule that passengers would take the first bus going their way tied in with more frequent services. However, soon there were also complaints of lack of internal room – the width of seats and gangway were less than on full-sized buses – and of lack of accommodation for luggage. Standards of driving, particularly where attempts were being made to run at higher speeds to take advantage of the possibility of the more nimble nature of smaller vehicles, were also apt to be criticised – minibus drivers were apt to be younger men, more prone to a 'boy racer' attitude, especially in competitive circumstances. However, the more general experience of minibuses tied in with that of deregulated services from 1986, which is outside the scope of this volume.

Standards of vehicle design did improve and while early NBC fleets of minibuses were on old-style Ford Transits (the model was just about to go out of production), the emphasis later switched more to the Mercedes-Benz L608D, which was larger and inevitably had a little of the 'superior' image of that make. In fact, the Transit proved to perform quite well, giving better reliability than might have been expected. Inevitably, clutch life on the manual gearbox model normally used was usually short, but replacement was simple and the cost of clutch parts or even exchange gearbox units was cheap, though some operators considered automatics a better bet overall.

The Mercedes-Benz was a heavier-duty model and soon earned a very good reputation, as well as being generally popular with drivers. I have driven several of the small Mercedes-Benz models as used for minibus or small coach duty and have always been impressed by the evidence of careful thought given to such matters as correctly-judged gear ratios which makes them a pleasure to drive despite the almost complete lack of the 'sophisticated' engineering apt to be associated with the make. Operators' maintenance experience has been good, though it seems ironic that the British commercial vehicle industry could not come up with anything as effective, for the Mercedes-Benz L608D and similar models are basically very simple and straightforward in design.

Frequent services using small-capacity buses were a departure from the trend of the previous 30 years or so, though the 20-seat Mercedes-Benz L608D was itself an early sign of a trend upwards once again from vehicles seating 16 passengers or even fewer. In Worcester, the local services were recast by Midland Red West in November 1985 with the entry into service of 60 of the L608D on nineteen routes, using Citibus as a fleetname.

Chapter Nine:
Variety without volume

One of the curious elements of the early 'eighties was the extent to which so depressing a period in terms of vehicle output was also one of numerous new names and models. Admittedly, at the beginning, the picture seemed relatively rosy, with only the single-deck bus side showing signs of depression, but the overall trend was downwards even then, as signalled on the bus side by the phasing out of the new bus grant and among coaches the inevitable response to the economic depression.

This seeming contradiction was nowhere more evident than among bodybuilders, when especially on the coach side new makers to the British market appeared almost every season, some not to continue for long. Among established firms, the overall trend was downwards, but there were quite marked variations. If integral vehicles are included, quite the most dramatic slide was that of the Leyland National. In four years, its deliveries to British operators were to be cut from the peak of 899 in 1978 to virtually a tenth of that, 92, in 1982, falling still lower to a mere 39 by 1984.

The leading coach bodybuilders showed a similar if less dramatic downward trend, though Plaxton held its leading position and managed to buck the overall trend in 1983 and in 1985 thanks largely to big NBC orders. The peak in that instance had been in 1979, when 1,356 coach plus 16 bus bodies had been built – by 1985 the total (including small numbers of Reeve Burgess bodies on midi-class chassis, that concern having been brought into the Plaxton empire by then) was 622. The slide at Duple was continuous, from 953 coaches and 34 buses in 1979, to a total of 203 in 1985. The take-over by the Hestair group in 1984 punctuated this decline but made little difference to the overall picture.

Among double-deck bodybuilders, the overall trend was also downwards, though from a later peak, and there was more variation. The 'integrals' (strictly the MCW Metrobus was barely in this class with its drivable underframe) showed their mutual inter-relationship, for as the Metrobus dropped from its peak output of 667 home-market deliveries in 1981 to fewer than half

that figure (311), the main reason was the 'political' switch of the 1982 London order entirely to the Titan. However, that was the only year when the Metrobus was not in the lead among 'bodywork'. Alexander was the beneficiary in 1982, delivering 342 double-deck bodies though even this was slightly down from 373 in 1981. Alexander had introduced a stylish new double-deck design, the R type, in 1980 and this may have marginally benefitted sales.

Eastern Coach Works also showed quite a big drop in double-deck deliveries in 1982 to 217, from 490 in 1981, as a consequence of NBC's sharp cut in new bus intake that year, but also recovered the following year. The other main bodybuilders were steadier, though nearly all had a good year in 1981, followed by a decline, though this was usually less sharp than had been experienced by the big producers. Northern Counties gradually slipped from building 211 double-deckers in 1981 to 156 in 1985, for example, and a similar slope at a lower level was followed by East Lancashire. Roe also

The end of one era, but the beginning of another. The closing-down of the Crossgates Works of Charles H. Roe as part of Leyland's attempt to slim down its capacity brought its position as main bus body supplier to West Yorkshire PTE and its largest predecessor, Leeds City Transport, to an end after a virtually unbroken run extending back 58 years. Two of the final batch of Leyland Olympians with coach seating, 5501 and 5502, placed in service in December 1984 and January 1985, are seen (left) on private hire duty in Morecambe in 1986. They had been completed by ECW, which itself was to survive only for another three years. As it turned out, Crossgates did not remain closed for long, being re-opened under the Optare banner. West Yorkshire County had supported the project and naturally the PTE was among the first customers. As well as further Olympians to almost identical design, a batch of Leyland Cub 33-seat midibuses, of which 1801 seen (right) was the first, was supplied during the winter of 1985-86.

dropped from 140, though the output in the final year, 1984, was actually up at 96 from the 78 the previous year. When Optare started trading from the former Roe premises in February 1985, the initial emphasis was on midi- and mini-buses, but ten double-deckers on Leyland Olympian chassis were among the vehicles ordered by West Yorkshire PTE.

A rather surprising if small-scale survivor through most of this period was Marshall, not a traditional double-deck bodybuilder, having made a start in this market in 1978 after its single-deck bus business had virtually collapsed due to the arrival on the scene of the Leyland National. It benefitted from the 1981 double-deck boom to the extent of 41 bodies in 1981, and although this was not sustained,

participation in the Volvo Citybus project – the prototype had a Marshall body – and subsequent orders, notably from Derby, kept output going in double figures, even if only just, until 1984.

Among single-deck buses, the downward slide was immense, though primarily related to NBC's quite remarkable cut-back in such vehicles. Traditionally, the major bus companies had purchased single-deckers on a much larger scale than any other type of operator. The decline had begun for NBC in the late 'seventies, triggered by the MAP changes in need, and already by 1980 the group's intake of such vehicles at a little over 300 vehicles was not much more than a third of what it had been during several years in the period up to 1976 – in 1973 the total single-deck bus intake of the group had

been 1,025 vehicles. Yet from 1982, the total dropped to around 50 per year, and in 1985 there were just 23, though by then the mini-bus intake, a mere eight in 1983, had grown to 485.

As already indicated, that drop was reflected in the total of Leyland National buses built, and in the early 'eighties it tended to be London Transport, PTE and other operators' interest in the model that kept the Workington production lines reasonably active, though a complete halt to output for periods of several weeks were not uncommon. Other single-deckers involved separate bodywork, and Alexander started as the largest builder involved, because of its position as supplier to SBG, but its needs for single-deckers fell too. Alexander never regained the total figure of 170 deliveries in Britain in

The Duple Dominant bus body outlived the coach body design of the same name, having been introduced two years later and having an agreeable non-dating quality about its appearance. Sales in the early 'eighties were limited by the low overall demand for single-deckers, but the type attracted a good share of what business was to be won. One of the more surprising orders was one for nine 51-seat buses on Leyland Tiger chassis for Midland Red (North), delivered in the earlier part of 1984. Up to a year or so earlier, there is no doubt that a heavy-duty bus requirement for NBC would have been fulfilled by Leyland National vehicles but the era of tight standardisation was ending. This operator had adopted a system of using local fleetnames in colour-keyed bands, in this case Mercian (light green) set against the standard NBC poppy red. Number 1709 is seen in Edgbaston Street, Birmingham, in August of that year.

1980, dropping as low as 23 in 1983 before recovering slightly. The other main contender was Duple with the Dominant bus design continuing to attract business from both independent and municipal users. The figures fluctuated rather, but Duple was usually first or second among body-on-chassis suppliers in this field even if the total only once crept above 50. The other outstanding performer was Wadham Stringer, previously largely in the welfare and ambulance field, which entered the market at an unpromising time in 1980, selling a single bus body that year but creeping upward to 30, second only to Duple's 31, in 1983 though being temporarily out of the bus market the following year.

Various other builders produced a few single-deck bodies during the early 'eighties, including East Lancashire, Marshall and Plaxton, though the last-mentioned's very high-waisted Bustler design failed to catch on, but that didn't affect the firm's position as the biggest bodybuilder in terms of home sales output because of its coaches. New firms Lex, which produced a rather angular design called the Maxeta, and Wright of Ballymena in Northern Ireland, built small numbers of bus bodies from 1981 and 1982 respectively.

However, it was on the coach side that real variety became evident. The various Continental producers of integral rear-engined models – Auwärter (Neoplan), Bova, Kässbohrer (Setra), MAN and Mercedes-Benz have already been mentioned. To them must be added Van Hool, which built both bodywork on chassis and integral vehicles, the latter coming on to the British market in 1982, when 33 of the total of 84 single-deckers were integrals,

Another, equally exceptional, case of the choice of the Leyland as the basis for a bus within an NBC fleet was that of East Midland Motor Services Ltd, which chose the Alexander P-type body then in production for a batch of nine 52-seat examples delivered in 1985. This body design was uncompromisingly angular in appearance and contrasted oddly with the curvaceous styles of earlier Alexander products. Number 625 is seen in Chesterfield in April of that year, soon after entering service.

plus two double-deck coaches. There were 41 single-deck and ten double-deck Van Hool integrals in 1983, but the numbers dwindled somewhat in later years, even though the total of single-deck Van Hool-bodied vehicles continued to rise, touching 201 in 1984 (including 26 integrals and two bus bodies for Hutchison of Overtown) falling back to 116 in 1985 – even so, this was sufficient to hold third place behind Plaxton and Duple. Jonckheere climbed from five in 1980 to 118 for both 1983 and 1984 and then fell to 78, taking fourth place latterly.

The main Continental body maker on the British market through the 'seventies, Caetano, dwindled in

numbers sold in the early 'eighties, from 69 in 1980 down to eleven in 1982, though there was a modest recovery to 35 in 1985. Also losing out, Willowbrook did considerable business with NBC for 1980 and 1981 but had difficulty in delivering the vehicles on time, a considerable proportion of the totals of 81, 61 and 73 delivered in the 1980 to 1982 years representing vehicles due in the previous years and once delivery of those outstanding was completed in mid-1982, output ceased, though the Loughborough factory did not close entirely and production restarted later.

In the early 'eighties, quite a number of Continental bodybuilders which had

Van Hool bodywork, built at Koningshooikt in Belgium, had been sold, at first in small numbers, in Britain since the early 'seventies, but integral coaches were also imported from 1982, including the impressive-looking Astromega six-wheel 12-metre double-decker. Southend Transport took delivery of three, with seats for 84 passengers for its express service to London and Heathrow – one is seen visiting London Transport's Chiswick works on an open day in July 1983, soon after entering service. These vehicles had rear-mounted Mercedes-Benz V8 engines, as also used on most of the Neoplan and Setra double-deckers.

their products in Britain appeared on the scene. One ̤o had already done so were ̤ading – Unicar had sold a total arly 90 of its distinctive body ̤gn over the 1979-80 period, but ̤ropped sharply in 1981 before vanishing until it reappeared in 1985. On the other hand, Ayats and Irizar, also from Spain, Padane, with a striking rather angular design, from Italy, and several of the numerous coach bodybuilders from the Low Countries appeared on the British market in the period around 1981-82. Some did not stay the course but others did well. The Dutch concern Berkhof brought one coach in for 1982, but then shot up to 48, 55 and 50 respectively in 1983-85, aided by its link with the Ensign Bus organisation with its contacts within the industry 'establishment' of that period as a major second-hand bus dealer – the choice of model names such as Esprite and Everest for Berkhof products in Britain reflected the link,

resulting in sales such as that to London Country of Berkhof Everest bodies for 30 Leyland Tigers, some being used on the Speedlink service between Heathrow and Gatwick airports run by Green Line.

From Belgium, LAG did moderately well, with sales at around 20 per year in 1983-85 including a few of an integral model, the Panoramic, but the Dutch Smit concern only sold small numbers. Van Rooijen, a concern associated with den Oudsten, the main bus bodybuilder for the Netherlands equivalent of NBC, introduced a striking design with raked windscreen in 1983, selling a few vehicles in the following years.

Against all this activity from Europe, British producers were having a difficult time, especially in relation to the declining market. Alexander could generally rely on at least a share of SBG coach orders, and also supplied part of NBC's requirements, notably during the latter's big 1983 coach fleet

programme, which lifted that year's Alexander coach sales above 50, though the total demand the following year dropped to fifteen. Generally, Alexander had been more at the dual-purpose end of the market and the T-type body in its original stepped-roof form dating from 1976 found only limited favour, but by the early 'eighties had been developed into more appealing TE (express) and TC styles.

An intriguing entry to the market was that of Wright of Ballymena, which introduced a coach called the Contour, which was far more adventurous in styling than might have been expected from a newcomer to coach bodywork from 1983. Sales, mainly on Bedford chassis, were modest, with an initial four that year and thirteen in 1984, but the firm obtained the benefit of the substantial Alusuisse concern's expertise on aluminium-alloy body structural design, and a foundation for later expansion had been laid.

A previously unknown name which began to figure among bus and coach bodybuilders supplying operators in Great Britain in the early 'eighties was Robert Wright & Son (Coachworks) Ltd, of Ballymena, Northern Ireland. At first it was associated with Bedford vehicles, and this YNQ model with angular-looking Wright 45-seat bus body was registered ABH 760X by the chassis maker before being sold via Shaw & Kilburn, an old-established Bedford dealer, to Maidstone Borough Council in 1982. It is seen in an advertising livery in July 1984, running by then as 260, having been renumbered from 160 in April 1983.

The contrast in the frontal appearance of another Wright-bodied Bedford in the Maidstone fleet could hardly be greater. After purchasing seven further Wright bus or dual-purpose bodies on YMT chassis, this example of the dramatically-styled Wright Contour coach design on a YNT chassis was added to the fleet, taking the fleet number 201, and is seen soon after delivery, in May 1984. The registration number shown was surrendered in favour of HKR 11 later in the year in the manner by then common for coaches – understandable as an effort to avoid the dating effect of the A-prefix, but a retreat from a particularly 'tidy' number.

Until the late 'seventies it was quite rare for most major British operators to purchase second-hand buses, unless acquired with a taken-over business, but in the 'eighties this began to be increasingly common. The London Transport fleet of Daimler or Leyland-built Fleetlines was very largely withdrawn from service in the period from 1979 into the early 'eighties and a high proportion saw further service. Midland Red was quite a large-scale buyer of many of them, including 2822, originally London Transport's DM1822, a CRL6 with MCW bodywork dating from 1975, seen here operating in the Leicester area in May 1982. As was quite often the case, the centre exit door had been removed and replaced with a standard window bay from another scrap vehicle, increasing the seating capacity from 71 to 74. When the Midland Red concern was split, these vehicles passed to Midland Red (East) which was soon renamed Midland Fox, and in 1984 the total of 77 ex-London Fleetlines formed the majority of that operator's double-deck fleet.

Chapter Ten:
Progress .... or disaster ?

The huge change in the character of the bus industry, both operating and manufacturing, during the mid-'eighties was very largely related to politics, yet by no means all could be traced directly to the new legislation or even the threat of it. There was a much broader underlying change, some of which had begun as a result of altering attitudes on the part of the Labour Government from 1976, as outlined in Chapter Two of the previous volume in this series, and events over even wider horizons.

The pressure of economics produced a need to contain subsidies which were growing for a combination of reasons – notably wider use of private cars, which made more services incapable of paying their way, and the open-ended nature of the new bus grant. Operators' purchases of what were, in effect, half-price buses made them more susceptible to elaboration in design and allowed manufacturers to put prices up by more

than inflation – British Leyland was itself under serious financial pressure and, in fairness, development costs were growing fast, partly as a result of more complex national and international legislation. It could also be argued that operators had been too willing to accept a need for more spare buses to cope with unreliability.

Even so, the atmosphere of centralisation of management, notably within NBC, the creation of bigger operating units and standardisation spilled over into the early 'eighties. It was like a tide, just about to turn yet still lapping slightly higher up the beach. Possibly the key example of high water mark, seeming fairly minor in itself, was the 1981 decision to put the headquarters of NBC's Maidstone & District and East Kent companies (with 547 and 430 buses respectively) which had been under common management since 1973, into common headquarters,

involving moving that of the former from its traditional address at Knightrider Street, Maidstone, to Canterbury. It seemed that a complete merger of these two companies was very much on the cards, yet it never happened.

On the contrary, operating companies began to be split into smaller units, initially related to county boundaries in many cases and reflecting the county council influence on many services. Midland Red had been a company akin to the proverbial 'mint with a hole' in its operating area since its services within the West Midlands county were transferred to West Midlands PTE in 1973. From September 1981, four area companies, named Midland Red (East) etc, took over, as mentioned in Chapter Four, plus one covering express services. The headquarters premises remained at Edgbaston, Birmingham, together with

The splitting of NBC subsidiaries into smaller units sometimes became quite complex. This 12-metre Leyland Leopard PSU5E/4 with ECW 57-seat bodywork was originally one of a batch supplied to Hants & Dorset Motor Services Ltd early in 1983, but passed to Shamrock & Rambler Coaches Ltd when H&D was split into smaller units on 1st April that year. A further split took place in January 1984, when the Southampton-based part of the business was transferred again to Pilgrim Coaches Ltd, which, with an 18-vehicle fleet, became NBC's smallest vehicle-operating subsidiary. It is seen in September of that year at Gloucester Green bus station in Oxford. Another vehicle of the same batch had the last Leopard chassis to be built for NBC. Pilgrim was sold in 1987 to Stagecoach together with Hampshire Bus (also formed from part of H&D), into which it was subsequently absorbed, and thus YEL 93Y changed ownership yet again.

Carlyle Works, which at that stage were still owned by the 'old' Midland Red company, though later converted into a separate business.

This principle gained momentum in 1983. From January, the Western National Omnibus Co Ltd was split into four companies. This time an echo of old names was introduced, for the familiar titles Devon General and Southern National appeared (though both had different operating areas to their predecessors and were, in fact, new companies), together with a new North Devon Ltd (using the fleetname Red Bus), while the new Western National Ltd was much smaller than its predecessor. Then in April 1983, Hants & Dorset Motor Services Ltd and the Gosport & Fareham Omnibus Co were split into new companies Hampshire Bus, Provincial (continuing the fleetname of Gosport & Fareham, though it also took over some of H&D's services in its area), Wilts & Dorset (reviving the fleetname of a company merged with H&D in 1969) and Shamrock & Rambler (another revival of an old fleetname, in this case of a Bournemouth-based coach operating concern that had been merged into National Travel in 1974).

In May 1983, the link between East Kent and Maidstone & District was unscrambled and, in addition, Hastings & District Transport Ltd appeared, taking over M&D operations in Hastings & Rye, echoing the old Hastings Tramways Co which had operated trolleybuses in the town and had been an M&D subsidiary from

1935 until 1957 (trolleybus operation had continued briefly directly under the M&D name until 1959). South Midland Ltd took over the country part of the City of Oxford Motor Services Ltd operations in August 1983; previously there had been a joint Oxford South Midland fleetname, though South Midland Motor Services Ltd had been a coach company with a rather complex history. In September 1983, the operations of the Bristol Omnibus Co Ltd from its Cheltenham, Gloucester, Stroud and Swindon depots were transferred to the new Cheltenham & Gloucester Omnibus Co Ltd.

The process of splits, ostensibly to form what were described as 'natural operating units' though by then with privatisation also in mind, continued. In January 1984, the Southampton part of Shamrock & Rambler Ltd was split further to become Pilgrim Coaches Ltd. In May 1984 the National Travel operating companies were split, the constituent parts reverting to old names in some cases, notably Black & White Motorways Ltd of Cheltenham and Wessex National Ltd at Bristol which between them took over from National Travel (West) in the south of England, whilst its northern fleet was taken over by Ribble, which thus reverted to running coach as well as bus operations. National Travel (East) became part of the West Riding group and National Travel (London) went to London Country Bus Services.

Later in the year, Eastern Counties split, Cambus Ltd taking over in the Cambridge area whilst coaches passed

to Ambassador Travel.

The full process of these and other related changes was very complex. Very often new companies were formed or existing 'shell' companies renamed, but in some cases long dormant companies were given fresh titles. Full details can be obtained from the table on page 358 of the *NBC Commemorative Volume*, which was one of the very many comprehensively researched contributions prepared by the late Keith Dickie.

An engineering revolution

Another feature of that period was the separation of the central engineering works which had formed part of most major operators into separate companies. This was part of a major change in the way NBC and other large concerns were maintaining their vehicles. Part of this was simply based on experience – on the whole, though modern vehicles were more complex and in some ways could be troublesome, there was no longer the same need for overhaul at regular intervals – methods of body construction gave better life, provided corrosion could be avoided, and mechanical units, for the most part, were longer-lived. In addition, a change in legislation triggered by an EEC Directive, 77/143, was ending the old system of a seven-year Certificate of Fitness issued by the Department of Transport on a new vehicle, with renewal for variable and usually shorter periods in its later life, linked to rather informal even though quite rigorous annual inspections. That had produced the custom of vehicles being given a major overhaul to coincide with the seven-year period and possibly again later in their lives. But from 1982 a more precise annual inspection was introduced and the C of F issued on initial inspection was for life.

Hence the concept of major overhauls no longer had the implied backing of officialdom. Central workshops were costly to run, apt to be more so as fleet sizes had shrunk and the facilities for vehicles needing less attention became excessive in relation to numbers of vehicles involved. A policy of making workshops financially independent, invoicing work done to operating departments, drew attention to this. Regrouping within NBC led to some closures, with vehicles from neighbouring companies being handled by what had become area workshops in some cases. In others, outside work began to be taken in and the workshops, often made into separate businesses in the course of the structural reorganisation of the bigger companies already mentioned, encouraged to think of themselves as being more independent.

This also applied to other organisations. London Transport had designed its Aldenham overhaul works, brought into use in the 'fifties, to deal with a fleet expected to reach 10,000 vehicles and planned to be able to handle up to 12,000, the older Chiswick premises concentrating largely on mechanical unit overhauls and the provision of staff training. By 1967, about a third of the Aldenham premises had been leased to Leyland as a service depot. In 1983, a review of the role of Chiswick and Aldenham was published by LT, and it concluded that neither works was economically viable, largely because of excessive overheads and outdated working practices – trade unions had always had a 'tight' attitude in LT. Closure of Aldenham and a drastic revision of practice at Chiswick was recommended. The matter became a political issue with Ken Livingstone and the Greater London Council, already at war with Nicholas Ridley and the Government; 'Red Ken' addressed a protest meeting. In due course, a joint review by LT and the unions was made – the outcome was agreement in 1984 for closure of some departments at Chiswick and an attempt at a survival plan for Aldenham – however, it did close in 1986, and Chiswick's future was increasingly in doubt even before that date.

The whole climate of involvement in bus engineering by major operators was changing. London Transport had decided in 1980 to drop its XRM project, originally for a four-axle double-decker with such features as hydrostatic transmission and 'active' suspension. A further proposal, the QRM, reviving the side-engined layout of the Q, was related to proposals for an MCW Metrobus Mark III which might have been available in such a form as an option to the more normal rear engine, but this too was dropped when LT gave MCW no share in its 1982 contract.

At NBC, it seems astonishing in retrospect to recall that there were plans to set up a vehicle manufacturing facility using Midland Red's Carlyle Works following the break with Leyland in 1982. The reasoning was concentrated on the Group's position in regard to single-deckers. There were 5,400 Leyland Nationals in service with NBC subsidiaries, and of these, 3,900 would be due for replacement by 1986. Even allowing for reduction in this number because of reduced need and wider use of coaches, it was considered that 2,000 vehicles would be needed at a rate of 285 per year over a seven-year period ending in 1993.

At the time, it was doubtless assumed that if NBC was to be privatised it would be as a complete organisation, while clearly the minibus was not then seen as a large-scale possibility. The original proposal was made in July 1982 by Peter Wyke Smith, NBC's Director of Engineering at the time. Barry Fox was put in charge of the project, became Chief Vehicle Development Engineer, and a 'Build A

Bus Scheme' (BABS) study w completed by August 1983. NBC w aware of Leyland's B60 project, to b announced the following year as the Lynx, but considered it expensive, especially as a surcharge would have been payable for NBC's choice of engine and transmission. A survey within the group led to the design of an 11-metre single-decker with Cummins LT10 and ZF transmission – a significant combination as far back as 1983-84, bearing in mind Leyland Bus adoption of both after privatisation. The plan was to build a prototype at Carlyle Works and then put the design out to tender for construction by vehicles makers, but by then the single-deck need within NBC and generally had collapsed and the project was dropped.

Attention turned to the development of a minibus, after the design team's brief involvement with conventional minibuses revealed many shortcomings in the models then of offer. 'Build A Minibus Investigation' (BAMBI) was for a vehicle in the 25-seat class of integral construction with Cummins or Perkins four-cylinder engine and manual or automatic transmission – this was approved as a design project in April 1985 and it was planned to build two prototypes by January 1986 but the plan to privatise NBC in individual company units caused it to be dropped, though subsequent commercial designs, notably the MCW Metrorider, showed evidence of its influence.

In some ways an opposite sign of the times was the use of Amalgamated Passenger Transport Ltd, a company that had handled the ex-railway interests in four joint committees involving

What had been the central workshops of NBC bus operating subsidiaries were converted into separate businesses and urged to become self-supporting. United Counties Engineering Ltd, formed in 1985, ran what had been the main works of the United Counties Omnibus Co Ltd in Northampton, but began, like several other similar organisations, to look for work from 'outside' concerns – seen here is a stand at a trade exhibition.

In 1981, NBC set up an organisation using the existing Amalgamated Passenger Transport Ltd company, to recover and recondition suitable engines and other units from withdrawn vehicles, as well as to provide general overhaul and repair facilities for the group's operating companies. At the time, vehicles like the Bristol RE single-deckers and Lodekka double-deckers seen being stripped in the background were being withdrawn in large numbers often more because of unsuitability for operating requirements than wear and tear, and it was logical to recover useful parts from them. Most of the numerous engines visible are Gardner or Leyland units.

municipal undertakings in Yorkshire in the 1969-74 period (see the earlier volume in this series, *Turbulent Times*) to operate a central engineering facility largely devoted to reclaiming engines, especially Gardner units, and semi-automatic gearboxes from withdrawn vehicles, overhauling them as well as units and vehicles from operating companies and supplying them back to the companies. It operated from September 1981 to October 1984 and was based at the former Lincolnshire Road Car Co Ltd central works at Bracebridge Heath, Lincoln. It was partly a legacy of contraction of the overall fleet and the fact that many buses withdrawn during that time had units of types still in use in vehicles that would be in service for some time.

Implementation of the Act

The build-up to deregulation and privatisation following the passing of the Transport Act 1985 extended through 1986 and in some respects even later and thus beyond the scope of this volume so far as detailed coverage

is concerned. However, in some respects, the story to be told is more of a continuation of what had gone before and cutting off even at 31st December 1985 would leave some untied ends of events told for the most part in this volume.

The passing of the Transport Act 1985 at the end of October of that year was the official signal for the steps it formalised to be put into effect, but much happened both before and after that date. The nature of Nicholas Ridley's views had been made clear from very soon after his appointment as Secretary of State for Transport two years earlier, and it was equally clear that they were likely to prevail, so the line of thought particularly within NBC had been related to the near-certainty of piecemeal privatisation as well as full deregulation long before the Act became law.

The ending of Lord Shepherd's term of office as NBC Chairman at the end of 1984 meant that a successor was needed and there were many people concerned for the future of the bus industry, far beyond the confines of NBC, who welcomed Robert Brook's appointment, for NBC had grown

steadily healthier during his period as Chief Executive from 1977. Here was a busman through and through, who would defend the true interests of the industry. Defend them he certainly tried to do, but the fact that he retained the post of Chief Executive was to prove a crippling handicap. As Chairman he was required to pursue the policies of the Board, increasingly under pressure from the Secretary of State; as Chief Executive he could advise against them, and it was impossible to do both at the same time. Robert Brook's own remarkably candid comment that he made a mistake in retaining the position of Chief Executive, with the result that 'I painted myself into a corner', is included in the interview with him in the *NBC Commemorative Volume*.

There was also a lot of irony in that NBC had turned itself round from being a loss-maker in some of its earlier years into being increasingly profitable from 1981 to 1983, and although the figures were not quite so good in 1984 and 1985, they were still firmly in the black. The directors understandably felt that the Company's achievements had made it 'pretty invincible'. Yet it can be argued that it had become *too* successful to be allowed to survive as a nationalised company. Its profitability demonstrated that it was saleable in one form or another and thus made it a prime candidate for privatisation. Perhaps even more crucial was that it offended against the idea that a publicly-owned organisation was inherently inefficient. In this connection its unexpected success against independent operators after coaching deregulation in 1980 was doubtless remembered with a kind of resentment by politicians who had staked their reputation on a contrary outcome.

On the other hand, the pressure of a more commercial approach, notably in the MAP reorganisations, had meant cuts in service and some unpopularity with the public. From that point of view, NBC probably did look big, rather dull and unresponsive, so talk of more flexible services from competitors had its electoral appeal.

The NBC board had supported the case made by the executives for the organisation to be sold as a single unit. The Government, and in particular Nicholas Ridley, not only ignored that advice but pressed that NBC should split its larger subsidiary companies to facilitate their sale. As indicated above, quite a number of subsidiaries had already been split, but the board felt that this was sufficiently mistaken in other cases to refuse. As a result, Nicholas Ridley issued a Directive on

The nature of the industry was altering rapidly in the early 'eighties, even if not yet as fundamentally as the more zealous right-wing politicians wanted. Just a year or two earlier, it would have been regarded as virtually impossible for a nationalised company to purchase coach bodywork from abroad, yet in 1983 East Kent was by no means alone in making such a departure for part of its requirements, even if in an unusual way. Although the photograph shown made good publicity material from selling tours to Holland, the vehicle was the first of a batch based on reconditioned AEC Reliance chassis dating from 1972 from which the original Duple Dominant bodywork had been replaced by new Berkhof Esprit, built in Valkenswaard, Holland. Number 8197 (reregistered A197 PPU by Ensign, the Berkhof agents, from HFN 28L) was completed in 1983 and a further nine similar rebuilds followed in 1984. The 'stripey' livery was as prescribed by NBC headquarters for the 1983 season, though the era of centralised control of such matters was itself coming to an end.

Opposition, or at the least strong unease, at the plans for deregulation and privatisation continued to be expressed by many within the industry during the period the legislation was passing through Parliament, even though it was obvious that with a clear majority the Government would have no difficulty in getting its Transport Bill through. This Preston Borough Council Leyland Atlantean was carrying lettering urging members of the public to 'save the buses' by contacting their MP in July 1985, but in October the Bill became an Act and the die was cast. The vehicle, No. 148, was one of a batch of ten of the AN68A/2R type with Alexander 82-seat two-door bodywork dating from early in 1980 – their arrival had allowed Preston's last examples of the front-engined Leyland Titan PD3 to be withdrawn from regular service. By 1984, Preston was running a fleet of 79 Atlantean AN68 buses with either East Lancs or Alexander bodywork, none more than ten years old and forming almost the entire fleet.

While the political turmoil was altering the climate in which the bus industry operated, some pointers to the future were to be found, though it would have required a clairvoyant to predict how far a modest-seeming business based in Perth might go. This Bristol Lodekka FLF seen in May 1981 had recently been acquired by a small firm with the fleetname Gloagtrotter, abbreviated to GT on vehicle sides. The name was derived from that of Robin and Ann Gloag, the latter better known in relation to the subsequent fleetname, Stagecoach, used at first primarily for its express services. Even then, the livery gave a hint of the style now familiar in many parts of Britain in the Stagecoach group fleets. The vehicle was one of a batch supplied to Central SMT in 1966, the ECW bodywork being of the 31ft.-long 76-seat type, with the rearmost side windows not as short as on the standard 70-seat version, favoured by the Scottish Bus Group.

By 1985, Stagecoach had expanded somewhat, but was still basically a local operator so far as bus services were concerned, though active in a still fairly modest way on long-distance services to London and within Scotland. When London Transport Routemasters began to be sold off, Stagecoach was among the first to acquire examples for further service, five being bought in January 1985 – the former RM1847, still in London livery but without fleetname, is seen in service with Stagecoach in Perth in August 1985. Though nominally 21 years old, it was still in good order, with only a few minor dents in the front dome – operators in various parts of Britain, including ex-NBC subsidiaries later bought by Stagecoach, were to purchase similar buses in large numbers in the following few years – the fast loading made possible by the provision of a conductor had new appeal in competitive operation.

13th February 1986, under powers included in the 1985 Act, requiring that United Automobile Services Ltd be divided into three parts (this was subsequently achieved by creating Northumbria Motor Services Ltd and transferring the southern part of the UAS area to East Yorkshire Motor Services Ltd); Ribble Motor Services Ltd into three parts (part went to a new subsidiary with an old name, North Western Road Car Co Ltd, though the new business was to be centred on Bootle, while the northern part of

Ribble's operations joined Cumberland Motor Services Ltd); Crosville Motor Services Ltd, two parts (the operations in Wales going to a new company, Crosville Wales Ltd), and London Country Bus Services Ltd into four parts (these were named London Country Bus Services (North West) Ltd and likewise for North East, South East and South West).

Robert Brook was increasingly unhappy about how the whole situation was going, recording that even before the episode of the Directive he was

beginning to take pleasure in failures to implement the policies he was entrusted to deliver. He also felt that senior NBC management was being shouldered out of the way. The Directive was to be implemented by 1st September, but long before this, Robert Brook resigned, with effect from 6th April 1986. It is probably fair to say that he could not tolerate the destruction of what he had built up. The 'steamroller' moved on inexorably and the very next day a further Directive from Mr Ridley required specifically that operating

One suspects that there may have been a certain perverse delight among staff who had served with the old North Western Road Car Co Ltd of Stockport (not least Robert Brook, NBC's increasingly unhappy Chairman and Chief Executive, who had been NWRCC's last General Manager in 1968-72), when the name was revived for a hived-off part of Ribble created against NBC's wishes, even though it was 'transplanted' about 35 miles westwards to Bootle. Here two ex-Ribble Leyland National 2 buses of the short 10.6-metre 44-seat type are seen at Maghull on 17th October 1986, just a few days before deregulation took effect. Number 308, the former Ribble 865 nearest the camera, is in the new company's livery, with diagonal stripes in the fashion of the time, and with promotional publicity on the side.

companies be sold off individually.

One further aspect of the implementation of the 1985 Act justifies mention as part of the complete change of atmosphere created for the new regime. During 1986, the procedure for deregulation went through its successive stages, the first being registration, by the end of February, of all those services operators intended to operate commercially during the first three months after D (for deregulation) day, 26th October 1986. These could not be altered except in special circumstances so as to allow the overall position to be evaluated by county councils and hence the need for subsidised services assessed. They were published by 1st April. By then, operators had discovered that deregulation did not mean freedom from bureaucracy and indeed were already finding the system in some ways more complex and actually less flexible than the old licensing system, which had allowed the Traffic Commissioners' offices to use their skill and knowledge with sensible discretion. There had been a series of leaflets issued under the name *Tomorrow's Buses* giving the impression of increased freedom – in principle, this was clearly so, since registration in general gave automatic authority, indeed obligation subject to 42 days' notice, to run whatever service was chosen, but in practice operators found some aspects alarmingly difficult.

In particular, the competition legislation came into effect from 26th July 1986, when the previous exemption to the Restrictive Trade Practices Act 1976 (from which the bus industry had been specifically excluded on the grounds that the Act was inappropriate) was lifted. Clearly, once again the fundamental differences between bus operation and other businesses were not regarded as important.

Understandably, in general, deals 'fixed up' between businesses normally expected to be competitive are apt to be viewed with suspicion – is the price being fixed at a higher level than would be arrived at by competition? The main problem in applying this to the bus industry lies in joint services. Most bus operators are surrounded by other concerns whose garages are likely to be in or near destinations of routes which may well be among the most important operated.

Traditionally, neighbouring companies would run such routes jointly, a system which makes the most economical use of the vehicles. Operator A sends the first bus from his garage at or near terminus A, bound for B, probably at the same time (chosen to suit travel needs of local people) as operator B departs from terminus B, bound for A. They work similarly throughout the day and the final journeys make for their respective home bases. The public gets an even gap between departures and the fare, traditionally, is nearly always the same in terms of pence per mile as other services in the area. What could be more logical and sensible? In half a century's study of the bus industry I can't think of a joint service that wasn't an asset to the travelling public.

In July 1986, a circular was issued on the new circumstances. It pointed out that 'any agreement between two or more people carrying on a business in the UK in which two or more parties accept some limitation on their commercial freedom' must be registered with the Office of Fair Trading. Running on the same routes with an agreed timetable as well as through ticketing were mentioned as coming within the terms of reference. It was, from then, illegal to operate an unregistered service. A registered service would be considered by the Office of Fair Trading for possible submission to the Restrictive Practices Court. It was left very vague as to the likelihood of such action, but the whole rather sour tone of the document conveyed the general impression that agreements were frowned upon.

Operators were left, deliberately it seemed, with the idea that joint operations would involve bureaucracy at the least and expensive court action as a distinct possibility. I feel that the bus industry was surprisingly complacent over this aspect of the 1985 Act. Reasonable competition is one thing, but the doctrinaire implication of the Department of Transport was that operators were expected to take an aggressive attitude towards each other. Gradually, over the following year or

One of the differences between bus or express coach operation and more general kinds of business is the way in which the routes are bound to link the headquarters or important bases of different companies. The concept of operating boundaries was supposed to be made obsolete in the directly competitive world of the new legislation but remains inevitable in practice. Here Plaxton-bodied Seddon Pennine VII ZS864 of Eastern Scottish, bound for Newcastle-upon-Tyne, in August 1980 is seen at Otterburn, a few miles after crossing the border into England and, by implication the territory of United Automobile Services Ltd, as it stood at that date. Joint operation of Newcastle-Edinburgh services had been established since long before Eastern Scottish (or its predecessor, SMT) and United came into common State ownership.

so, we were into the world of 'bus wars', and 'attacks' on existing services, quite deliberately intended to undermine an existing facility and hence causing waste in the use of valuable assets.

Inevitably, there are winners and losers in such situations, and the losers rarely continue for long. Hence there is a tendency for continuous change, with constantly altering services and route variations. Where two or more operators cover the same route, they are apt to try to 'attack' each other by running within a few minutes of each other, followed by a long gap. Is this progress? There is clear evidence in the Manchester area, to take an example which could doubtless be repeated in many other places, that passengers have become so fed up with frequently changing bus services that they have begun to switch to trains, whose routes cannot alter in any normal time-span and whose timetables are also generally not subject to frequent change. Could this be the real secret weapon favouring rapid transit rail systems, though their huge cost makes even the most generous bus service cheap?

In the past, competition between operators was almost invariably resolved either by take-over or an operating agreement of one kind or another. In my view, the latter was often the more favourable outcome for the public.

Current legislation is based on the premise that the continuance of competition is itself desirable. Operators are told, in effect, not to make agreements and even, in some cases, to divest themselves of taken-over businesses. So the unfortunate passengers seem to be condemned to an endless limbo of competition followed by collapse of one party, and then another round of competition until there is a further collapse, and so on *ad infinitum*. While this goes on, no one dares to invest in new rolling stock and operators are so weakened by the process that they probably cannot afford to in any case.

Implications for manufacturers

And what of the vehicles? Operators constantly under the threat of attack, even when it is not actually occurring are hardly encouraged to invest the large sums needed to buy new vehicles. Indeed such an investment has to be underpinned by a reasonable level of assurance that the buses can earn their keep over quite a lengthy period. But if operators are liable to discover, at no more than six weeks' notice, that a horde of minibuses or cheaply-bought old larger buses is liable to try and skim off the revenue from their most important routes, it may seem unwise to commit resources or take on loan charges on new vehicles.

When Nicholas Ridley addressed the Bus & Coach Council at Blackpool in September 1984, he said that current forecasts implied that there would be a drop in orders but this would be followed by an increase. There were jeers from the audience and a shout of "Rubbish!". It came from David Hargreaves, at that time Chairman of both the Duple and Dennis concerns, who pointed out that, under the policies of the Government, annual bus (excluding coach) deliveries to the UK market had dropped from 3,300 in 1979 to 1,100. Export achievements would be lost in the absence of a firm home market. Mr Ridley conceded that these figures were alarming but considered that if there were an increase of imports it would be up to the manufacturing industry to adapt, perhaps by turning to lighter types of bus.

Well, it is true that minibus demand went up, though the artificial peak in 1986-87 resulting from NBC's decision to back the type heavily has not been repeated subsequently. But the British bus and coach manufacturing industry, once the world leader in terms of exports as well as respect for the quality of its designs, has suffered mightily. By February 1987, I was asking the question whether this country was heading for a 'third world' type of transport industry in an article for *Coaching Journal*, with total sales of full-sized buses and coaches in the UK down to 2,141 for 1986, of which 1,503 were of British origin – in 1979, the Leyland group alone had sold 3,408, down to 873 in 1986.

Leyland Bus did not survive very long as an independent management

Victoria Coach Station in London had been a scene of success for the National Bus Company in the period from the autumn of 1980, when coach deregulation resulted in an expansion of express services, largely because the restrictions that had previously applied because of railway objections were removed. The building was modified, gaining an extra layer of offices at the top to provide extra accommodation, partly to be rented out commercially but also to allow the NBC headquarters to move from New Street Square in October 1982
. However, in the following few years the air of self-confidence that had been built up ebbed away as Government policy turned not merely to the privatisation of NBC but an insistence on its dismemberment. It is sometimes said that the organisation had proved too successful as a nationalised concern to be allowed to survive. The coach seen in this view is United Automobile Services No. 171, an example of the Plaxton 4000 double-decker, built on a Neoplan underframe as used for the Skyliner model, but combined with Plaxton-built bodywork, one of a pair placed in service in the summer of 1985 on services from Peterlee and Hartlepool to London. They were equipped to Rapide specification, with seats for 71 passengers.

As matters stood in the mid-'eighties, Dennis seemed likely to be one of the more vulnerable manufacturers in the prevailing atmosphere of an alarming drop in demand and uncertainty about the future – moreover it had a history of uncertainty, bus production having ceased more than once and faltered several times over the years. Who could have foreseen that by 1992, it would be the only major British-owned bus chassis manufacturer and the only one with its factory in England? Hyndburn Borough Transport had been one of the local authority users which turned to Dennis in the early 'eighties – not for the first time, for Dennis buses had been favoured by what was then the Accrington undertaking in the 1928-29 period. Seen here is No. 51 (B51 XFV), one of a pair of Dennis Falcon HC type single-deckers in rare short-wheelbase form placed in service in 1985 – the 43-seat bodywork by East Lancs was fitted with dual-purpose seating to give a more coach-like interior, an increasingly common practice in the run up to deregulation.

'Threatened by the Transport Bill ...' read the poster on the side of this West Midlands PTE MCW Metrobus as it ran down New Town Row in Birmingham in September 1985. The reference was to the effect of the legislation on local services but as it turned out, it could also have been read to apply to the make of bus, and indeed much of Britain's bus manufacturing industry. The MCW concern, or its predecessor, Metropolitan-Cammell, had been the most influential pioneer of metal-framed bus bodywork in Britain and the greater part of the municipal and PTE buses running in Birmingham, like those in many other fleets, had been built in its works in the city. The Metrobus, MCW's first venture in the manufacture of a complete bus designed as well as built in its own premises, had proved immensely successful – over 2,000 had been built by the time WMPTE's 2683 had entered service in 1983, and even after the exceptional peak demand of 1980-81 about 400 per year were still being built for British operators in 1982-85. Yet even the promising, if in some ways under-developed, Metrorider minibus could not save the firm, starved of orders in the climate created by the Transport Act 1965, as it became, and production ceased in 1988, though Optare picked up some of the pieces.

buy-out after being privatised, being sold to Volvo in 1988, with high hopes for expansion, since cruelly dashed.

Of the rest of the major British bus makers as they stood in 1985, MCW, once so promising, has gone; Bedford, already struggling, has also vanished, and Ford was already dead in this field, except in minibuses. Only Dennis still stands as an independent British-owned bus chassis maker and, indeed, is soon to be the only major such works in England, but the other company David Hargreaves spoke for in 1984, Duple, is another of the casualties, Plaxton now being the only large British coach body maker. Among the bus bodybuilders, we are nowadays down to Alexander, with Northern Counties fighting back after being on the brink of closure as this goes to press, and East Lancashire

now virtually the only instance of a manufacturer with links to an operating group because of its Drawlane connections. Optare, with considerable promise as well as its inheritance by purchase of parts of MCW's market is now part of the United Buses empire with DAF as its central power base in Holland.

Leyland's once proud role, not only as Britain's biggest bus manufacturer, supplying most of the nation's needs, but also a world-beating exporter, has dwindled to the incredible position that, as this volume goes to press, its Workington factory, the last remaining and most modern of its bus-building facilities, is on the point of closure. All that is left of Leyland is the production of the highly successful Olympian double-deck chassis at Volvo's Scottish

truck factory at Irvine – almost literally a mere ghost of the past.

Both Volvo and DAF are well-run manufacturers of high integrity, but it is tragic, even so, that the key decisions affecting so much of what is left of the manufacturing industry are made in Sweden or Holland rather than in Britain.

Can both the operating and manufacturing sides of the industry be turned round before it is too late? It is significant that it is the big operators such as the Stagecoach group, West Midlands Travel and some of those run on more traditional lines such as Lothian Region Transport, that have been able to place healthy orders for new buses.

Epilogue – and some thoughts for the future

The historian has the rather unfair advantage of hindsight in commenting on past events, for those who took the key decisions at the time could only work on the basis of their own experience and beliefs. Even so, we must all accept the judgement of history in one way or another, and writers' words are there for all to examine and see whether they were right or wrong, years later!

On this basis, it is not difficult to conclude that, had NBC not succeeded in meeting the Conservative Government's pressure that it should become profitable in the early 'eighties, it might have survived for longer in much the same way as does British Rail, still State-owned and supported by subsidy. However, given the level of success as measured in that way by 1983, it does seem ironical that its complete dismemberment and the heavy emphasis on deregulation was triggered by the revelation of Cecil Parkinson's extra-marital activities and the consequent Cabinet reshuffle which put Nicholas Ridley into the driving seat as Secretary of State for Transport.

Bearing in mind Mr Ridley's antagonism to Britain's closer involvement with Europe, it is equally ironic that deregulation and the internecine competition of bus operators, in which he so passionately believed, has resulted in most of Britain's bus manufacturing industry, starved of orders, either being closed or falling into foreign ownership. In particular, the most popular make of minibus – another concept he favoured – has proved to be Mercedes-Benz. This is completely justifiable in the sense that models of this make have proved very effective (though it is sad that no British firm was able to offer anything as well regarded), but hardly in keeping with Mr Ridley's well-known anti-German views, which ultimately led to his departure from the Government.

However, it is more important to consider what should be done in the future. At the time of writing, it is still impossible to predict a clear outcome for the April 1992 General Election. What is more, though the general slant of the three main political parties is obvious, none has spelled out a comprehensive plan for developing public transport – indeed bus services have been barely even mentioned.

The shift of the general pattern of political thought was so great in the 'eighties that all three parties seem to have swallowed the idea that competition is desirable, albeit to varying degrees. In one sense it is inevitable, but the main competitor to any form of public transport within Britain is bound to remain the car, and there is a strong case for the revival of a word all too rarely heard nowadays – co-ordination. Simply allowing, even encouraging, bus operators to seek to deliberately damage each other by drawing away business can only lead to more bankruptcies, a general impoverishment of the whole industry's structure, and, in all probability, the complete demise of the bus and coach manufacturing industry which supplied 95 per cent of the nation's needs in 1979. An easily applied first step would be the withdrawal of the impediments to joint operation of services.

Instead of applying deregulation to the one area where it has been excluded so far, London, there is a case for adopting the tendering system used in the capital more widely. It has the great virtue of giving the firm successful in obtaining a contract sufficient financial stability to enable it to provide up-to-date buses, and indeed of requiring this as a condition of the contract. Thus far the idea has only been applied on a limited scale, but more general application would be possible if Mrs Lynda Chalker's 1984 proposal of selecting operators for profitable routes by a form of tendering in which the highest premium, subject to a quality threshold, would be sought. The funds obtained would be available to help support unprofitable but socially desirable routes – in other words, providing a means of devoting part of the profits from good services to help in providing a satisfactory overall network of routes. Clearly this system of cross-subsidy could develop into a form of network franchising.

It has been suggested that it is apt to take about 60 years for the good ideas of the past to come back into favour again, an example being the idea of the economist, J. M. Keynes, now coming back into favour. On this basis, perhaps road service licensing is due for re-examination. The system based on the Road Traffic Act 1930 and used until the early 'eighties had its faults – such as a tendency to simply perpetuate the routes and operators in existence at the beginning, with almost a 'closed shop' against newcomers, though even this enabled fleets to be kept up-to-date in a way not seen today. Maybe its biggest fault was the 'remoteness' of the Traffic Commissioners and their offices – most bus users were quite unaware of them, despite their value as, in effect, ombudsmen to protect the public.

Maybe there would be merit in constructing a system combining many of the functions of the Traffic Commissioners as they stood until 1980 with those of the Passenger Transport Executives as they now stand within the former Metropolitan counties, but broadened further to oversee the provision of public transport, perhaps including rail as well as road, on an area basis over the whole country. They would need to be powerful enough to be able to demand high standards from operators, whether large or small, yet should also be approachable by the public – maybe there should again be an 'electable' element. It is time for serious thought and rapid action.

Index

Acknowledgements

In writing each of these volumes, I think back to the people with whom I came in contact during the period in question as well as those with whom I have talked or corresponded on relevant subjects since. They would make a huge list, quite impossible to acknowledge individually, and yet even brief conversations added to the overall picture.

At the end of 1979, I left my position as Technical Executive with the Confederation of British Road Passenger Transport (CPT, later known as the Bus and Coach Council) to devote my time to becoming a writer, mainly as an author and editor of books published by TPC but also writing articles for the technical press, though for a little while I continued to do some work on a part-time basis for CPT. This combination of duties brought me in contact with many people in the industry, quite a high proportion of whom I had known for longer periods – up to 30 years in some cases.

A broader dimension to this, mainly relating to the coach side of the business was the work I did for *Coaching Journal* (though its secondary title, *Bus Review* gave an indication of its coverage on that side, too), for which I acted as Technical Editor.

I owe a debt of gratitude to all of the organisations already mentioned and it is difficult to be fair in pinpointing individuals but people who particularly come to mind in that period include Alan Gurley, both before and after he moved from NBC to become CPT's Technical Director; all my friends at TPC, not least John Senior, without whose vision a whole breed of books about buses would never have come into existence; the three Johns at Coaching Journal – the late John Speed, John Fielder and John Taylor, and management, engineering and publicity staff of various manufacturing and operating concerns.

Further insight into the events of the early 'eighties was to come from subsequent contact with other friends, perhaps most notably the authors of the NBC commemorative volume, with whom I worked for about eighteen months in 1988-89. John Birks, the leader of that team, as well as having a keen interest in transport history himself, had been Chief Executive Officer of National Express in 1979-84. The late Keith Dickie, as well as being agreeably hospitable by allowing me to share his office on my frequent visits to Oxford, proved to be a fountain of knowledge on the complex restructuring of NBC, as evidenced by the meticulous charts of the company histories in that volume. I had known Tony Beetham since his appointment as General Manager of City of Oxford Motor Services Ltd in 1969, and he and Yvonne Britten, as well as Keith, had extensive knowledge of NBC from the perspective of the Planning department. It was enlightening to see NBC's organisation from the inside, even if retrospectively – thoroughly professional if a little bureaucratic, perhaps.

In a more immediate sense I must give my usual, but none the less sincere, thanks to the team at TPC who convert my words into the finished product, not least Carolyn, Margaret and Shirley. Photographers who were particularly helpful included David Wayman, Roy Marshall, Geoff Atkins, Max Fowler, Michael Fowler and Stewart Brown.

Bibliography

Even the technical press became caught up in the upheaval of the industry in the 'eighties. Both *Commercial Motor* and *Motor Transport*, perhaps influenced by an upsurge in goods as opposed to passenger transport, tended to diminish their coverage of the bus industry – ultimately *Motor Transport* gave up bus and coach content completely in 1986, just as deregulation was about to come into effect. This vacuum was filled on the bus side by the creation of *Bus Business* in May of that year, though strictly speaking that falls outside the timespan of this volume.

My own involvement with the technical press during the period was as a contributor and then Technical Editor of *Coaching Journal* on a part-time basis, so my recommendation of it as a handy reference source on vehicle design may be biased, but the old days of a whole range of substantial monthly trade magazines had long gone. *Buses* continued to be the standard source for fleet news, blossoming into a larger page size from July 1980, and *The Omnibus Magazine* contained other useful material, not least Paul Heel's annual reviews of deliveries of chassis and bodywork.

TPC publications over the years makes up a library of their own, some inevitably out of print. However, notable among recent publications with material relevant to the early 'eighties are the substantial *NBC commemorative volume* mentioned under my acknowledgements, *Glasgow Buses*, *Liverpool Transport Volume V*, *Forty Years with London Transport* and the *Shearings history*. Noteworthy among other books of interest in relation to the period is Paul E. Garbutt's *London Transport and the Politicians*.